Contents

MEAT

VEGETARIAN

DESSERTS

Carrot & Coriander Soup

Coriander adds a lively flavour to this warming winter soup made from basic ingredients.

ingredients

SERVES FOUR

- 50g/2oz/4 tbsp butter
- 2 leeks, sliced
- 450g/1lb carrots, sliced
- 15ml/1 tbsp ground coriander
- 1.2 litres/2 pints/5 cups chicken stock
- 150ml/¼ pint/⅔ cup Greek (US strained plain) yogurt
- salt and ground black pepper
- 30–45ml/2–3 tbsp chopped fresh coriander (cilantro), to garnish

cook's tip

Use home-made stock to add a great depth of flavour.

1 Melt the butter in a large pan over low heat. Add the sliced leeks and carrots and stir well, coating the vegetables with the butter. Cover with a tight-fitting lid and continue to cook gently for about 10 minutes until the vegetables are just beginning to soften, but do not let them colour.

variation

For a vegetarian version of this soup, substitute a good quality vegetable stock or water for the chicken stock.

2 Stir the ground coriander into the vegetables and cook for about 1 minute. Pour in the stock and season to taste with salt and pepper. Bring to the boil, cover and simmer for about 20 minutes, until the leeks and carrots are tender.

3 Leave to cool slightly, then ladle the soup into a blender or food processor, in batches if necessary, and process until smooth. Return the soup to the pan and add about 30ml/2 tbsp of the yogurt, then taste the soup and adjust the seasoning again to taste. Reheat gently but do not boil.

4 Ladle the soup into bowls and put a spoonful of the remaining yogurt in the centre of each bowl. Sprinkle with the fresh coriander sprigs and serve immediately.

NUTRITIONAL INFORMATION: Energy 195kcal/807kJ; Protein 4.6g; Carbohydrate 12.3g, of which sugars 11.1g; Fat 14.9g, of which saturates 8.7g; Cholesterol 27mg; Calcium 108mg; Fibre 4.3g; Sodium 132mg.

Leek & Rocket Soup

The distinctive peppery taste of rocket is wonderful in this filling soup, thickened with potato.

ingredients

SERVES FOUR TO SIX

- 50g/2oz/4 tbsp butter
- 1 onion, chopped
- 3 leeks, chopped
- 2 medium-sized potatoes, diced
- 900ml/1½ pints/3¾ cups light chicken or vegetable stock
- 2 large handfuls rocket (arugula), coarsely chopped
- 150ml/¼ pint/⅔ cup double (heavy) cream
- salt and ground black pepper
- garlic-flavoured ciabatta croûtons, to serve

1 Melt the butter in a large heavy pan over low heat. Add the onion, leeks and potatoes and stir until all the vegetable pieces are well coated in butter.

2 Cover with a tight-fitting lid and cook for about 15 minutes until the vegetables are just beginning to soften, but do not let them colour.

3 Pour in the stock, bring to the boil and cover again, then simmer for a further 20 minutes, until the vegetables are tender.

4 Press the soup through a sieve (strainer) or food mill and return to the rinsed-out pan. (When puréeing the soup, don't use a blender or food processor, as these will give the soup a gluey texture.) Add the chopped rocket, stir in and cook gently for about 5 minutes.

cook's tip

To make the croûtons, cut the bread into 1cm/½in cubes, removing the crust, and toss with olive oil and a crushed garlic clove. Bake in a roasting pan.

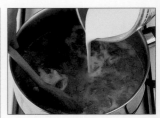

5 Stir the cream into the soup, then season to taste with salt and pepper. Reheat gently but do not allow to boil. Ladle the soup into warmed bowls, sprinkle a few ciabatta croûtons into each one and serve immediately.

NUTRITIONAL INFORMATION: Energy 245kcal/1015kJ; Protein 3g; Carbohydrate 11.9g, of which sugars 3.7g; Fat 20.9g, of which saturates 12.8g; Cholesterol 52mg; Calcium 54mg; Fibre 2.7g; Sodium 75mg.

Tomato & Basil Soup

In the summer, when tomatoes are both plentiful and inexpensive, this is a lovely soup to make.

ingredients

SERVES FOUR

- 30ml/2 tbsp olive oil
- 1 onion, chopped
- 2.5ml/½ tsp caster (superfine) sugar
- 1 carrot, finely chopped
- 1 potato, finely chopped
- 1 garlic clove, crushed
- 675g/1½lb ripe tomatoes, coarsely chopped
- 5ml/1 tsp tomato purée (paste)
- 1 bay leaf
- 1 sprig fresh thyme
- 1 sprig fresh oregano
- 4 fresh basil leaves, coarsely torn
- 300ml/½ pint/1¼ cups light chicken or vegetable stock
- 2–3 pieces sun-dried tomatoes in oil, drained
- salt and ground black pepper
- basil leaves, for garnishing

1 Heat the oil in a large pan over low heat. Add the onion, sprinkle with the sugar and cook gently for 5 minutes.

2 Add the chopped carrot and potato, stir well, then cover the pan with a tight-fitting lid and cook gently for a further 10 minutes until the vegetables are beginning to soften, but do not let them colour.

3 Stir in the garlic, tomatoes, tomato purée, bay leaf, thyme and oregano sprigs torn basil leaves and stock and season to taste with salt and pepper. Cover the pan again with the lid and simmer gently for 25–30 minutes, or until the vegetables are tender.

4 Remove the pan from the heat and press the soup through a sieve (strainer) to extract all the skins and seeds of the tomatoes and the herb stems. Taste the soup and season with salt and pepper.

5 Return the soup to the rinsed-out pan and reheat gently, then ladle into four warmed soup bowls. Finely chop the sun-dried tomatoes and mix with a little oil from the jar. Add a spoonful to each serving, then sprinkle with basil leaves and serve at once.

cook's tip

Tear basil, as cutting bruises the leaves and spoils the flavour.

NUTRITIONAL INFORMATION: Energy 129kcal.538kJ; Protein 2.2g; Carbohydrate 13.4g, of which sugars 9.2g; Fat 7.8g, of which saturates 1.3g; Cholesterol 0mg; Calcium 26mg; Fibre 3g; Sodium 30mg.

Minestrone with Pesto

This hearty, Italian mixed vegetable soup is a great way to use up any leftover vegetables.

ingredients

SERVES FOUR

- 1 onion
- 2 celery sticks
- 1 large carrot
- 45ml/3 tbsp olive oil
- 150g/5oz French (green) beans, cut into 5cm/2in pieces
- 1 courgette (zucchini), thinly sliced
- 1 potato, cut into 1cm/½in cubes
- ¼ Savoy cabbage, shredded
- 1 small aubergine (eggplant), cut into 1cm/½in cubes
- 200g/7oz can cannellini beans, drained and rinsed
- 2 Italian plum tomatoes, chopped
- 1.2 litres/2 pints/5 cups stock
- 90g/3½oz dried vermicelli
- salt and ground black pepper

For the pesto

- about 20 fresh basil leaves
- 1 garlic clove
- 10ml/2 tsp pine nuts
- 15ml/1 tbsp grated Parmesan cheese
- 15ml/1 tbsp grated Pecorino cheese
- 30ml/2 tbsp olive oil

1 Chop the onion, celery and carrot finely. Heat the oil in a large pan, add the chopped mixture and cook over a low heat, stirring, for 5–7 minutes.

2 Mix in the French beans, courgette, potato and cabbage. Stir-fry over a medium heat for 3 minutes. Add the aubergine, cannellini beans and tomatoes, and stir-fry for 2–3 minutes more. Pour in the stock with salt and pepper to taste. Bring to the boil. Stir well, cover and lower the heat. Simmer for 40 minutes.

3 To make the pesto, process all the pesto ingredients in a food processor until the mixture forms a smooth sauce, adding 15–45ml/1–3 tbsp water through the feeder tube if necessary.

4 Break the pasta into small pieces and add it to the soup. Simmer, stirring frequently, for 5 minutes. Add the pesto sauce and stir it in well, then simmer for 2–3 minutes more, or until the pasta is al dente. Taste for seasoning. Serve hot, in warmed soup plates or bowls.

NUTRITIONAL INFORMATION: Energy 387kcal/1618kJ; Protein 13.1g; Carbohydrate 40g, of which sugars 9.6g; Fat 20.6g, of which saturates 4g; Cholesterol 8mg; Calcium 173mg; Fibre 7.7g; Sodium 527mg.

French Onion Soup

This rich, dark brown version of onion soup is the absolute classic recipe from France.

ingredients

SERVES FOUR

- 25g/1oz/2 tbsp butter
- 15ml/1 tbsp sunflower oil
- 3 large onions, thinly sliced
- 5ml/1 tsp soft dark brown sugar
- 15g/½ oz/1 tbsp plain (all-purpose) flour
- 2 x 300g/10oz cans condensed beef consommé
- 30ml/2 tbsp medium sherry
- 10ml/2 tsp Worcestershire sauce
- 8 slices French bread
- 15ml/1 tbsp French coarse-grained mustard
- 75g/3oz Gruyère cheese, grated
- salt and ground black pepper
- 15ml/1 tbsp chopped fresh thyme, to garnish

1 Heat the butter and oil in a large pan over low heat. Add the onions and brown sugar and cook gently, stirring occasionally, for at least 20 minutes, until the onions start to brown and caramelize.

2 Stir in the flour and cook, stirring, for a further 2 minutes. Pour in the consommé and two cans of water, then add the sherry and Worcestershire sauce. Season with salt and pepper, cover with a tight-fitting lid and simmer gently for 25–30 minutes.

3 Preheat the grill (broiler) and, just before you are ready to serve, toast the bread lightly on both sides. Spread one side of each slice with the mustard and top with the grated cheese. Grill (broil) the toasts until the cheese has melted and is bubbling and golden.

cook's tip

Depending on the variety of onion you are using, you may need to cook them for longer than 20 minutes to get them really soft and caramelized.

4 Ladle the soup into warmed soup bowls. Place two slices of toasted bread topped with cheese on top of each bowl of soup and sprinkle with chopped fresh parsley to garnish. Alternatively, place two slices of toasted bread in the base of each bowl and ladle the soup over them, then garnish with chopped thyme. Serve the soup immediately.

NUTRITIONAL INFORMATION: Energy 415kcal/1745kJ; Protein 13g; Carbohydrate 61.6g, of which sugars 12.6g; Fat 14.1g, of which saturates 6.7g; Cholesterol 25mg; Calcium 240mg; Fibre 4.1g; Sodium 1022mg.

Curried Parsnip Soup

The spices in this soup impart a delicious, mild curry flavour, which is very warming.

ingredients

SERVES FOUR

- 25g/1oz/2 tbsp butter
- 1 garlic clove, crushed
- 1 onion, chopped
- 5ml/1 tsp ground cumin
- 5ml/1 tsp ground coriander
- 450g/1lb (about 4) parsnips, sliced
- 10ml/2 tsp medium curry paste
- 450ml/¾ pint/scant 2 cups well-flavoured chicken or vegetable stock
- 450ml/¾ pint/scant 2 cups milk
- 60ml/4 tbsp sour cream or crème fraîche
- good squeeze of lemon juice
- salt and ground black pepper
- 1 naan, lightly fried and cut into small dice, to serve
- toasted sesame seeds, to garnish

1 Heat the butter in a large pan over medium heat. Add the garlic and onion and cook, stirring occasionally, for 4–5 minutes, until lightly golden. Stir in the cumin and coriander and cook, stirring frequently, for a further 1–2 minutes.

2 Add the parsnips and stir until well coated with the butter, then stir in the curry paste, followed by the stock. Bring to the boil, then reduce the heat to low, cover with a tight-fitting lid and simmer gently for 15 minutes.

3 Check that the parsnips are tender, then leave the soup to cool slightly before ladling it into a blender or food processor, in batches if necessary, and processing to a smooth purée.

4 Return the soup to the rinsed-out pan, stir in the milk and heat gently, without boiling, for 2–3 minutes.

5 Stir in 30ml/2 tbsp of the sour cream or crème fraîche and lemon juice to taste. Season the soup to taste with salt and pepper.

6 Ladle the hot soup into warmed bowls and top each serving with a generous spoonful of the remaining sour cream or crème fraîche. Serve immediately with a handful of lightly fried naan croutons and garnish with a sprinkling of toasted sesame seeds

NUTRITIONAL INFORMATION: Energy 207kcal/865kJ; Protein 6.5g; Carbohydrate 21.2g, of which sugars 13.2g; Fat 11.3g, of which saturates 6.6g; Cholesterol 29mg; Calcium 200mg; Fibre 5.4g; Sodium 104mg.

Pasta & Chickpea Soup

The addition of fresh rosemary gives this robust soup a typically Mediterranean flavour.

ingredients

SERVES FOUR TO SIX

- 1 onion, 2 carrots
- 2 celery sticks
- 60ml/4 tbsp olive oil
- 400g/14oz can chickpeas, rinsed and drained
- 200g/7oz can cannellini beans, rinsed and drained
- 150ml/¼ pint/⅔ cup passata
- 120ml/4fl oz/½ cup water
- 1.5 litres/2½ pints/6¼ cups vegetable or chicken stock
- 2 fresh rosemary sprigs
- 200g/7oz/scant 2 cups dried conchiglie
- salt and ground black pepper
- Parmesan cheese, to serve

1 Chop the onion, carrots and celery finely, either by hand or in a food processor.

2 Heat the oil in a large heavy pan, add the chopped vegetable mixture and cook over a low heat, stirring frequently, for approximately 5–7 minutes.

3 Add the chickpeas and cannellini beans, stir well to mix, then cook for 5 minutes. Stir in the passata and water. Cook, stirring frequently, for 2–3 minutes.

4 Add 475ml/16fl oz/2 cups of the vegetable or chicken stock, one of the rosemary sprigs and salt and pepper to taste. Bring to the boil, cover, then simmer gently, stirring occasionally, for 1 hour.

5 Pour in the remaining stock, add the pasta and gradually bring to the boil, stirring occasionally. Lower the heat and simmer, stirring frequently, for approximately 7–8 minutes or according to the instructions on the packet, until the pasta is *al dente*.

6 Taste for seasoning. Remove the rosemary sprig and serve the soup hot, in warmed soup bowls, topped with grated Parmesan cheese and a few rosemary leaves.

variations

· You can use other pasta shapes, but conchiglie are ideal because they scoop up the chickpeas and beans.

· If you like, crush 1–2 garlic cloves and 50g/2oz/¼ cup diced pancetta or smoked bacon and fry them with the vegetables.

NUTRITIONAL INFORMATION: Energy 271kcal/1151kJ; Protein 13.9g; Carbohydrate 50.3g, of which sugars 6.4g; Fat 3g, of which saturates 0.4g; Cholesterol 0mg; Calcium 98mg; Fibre 8.6g; Sodium 476mg.

Mixed Bean Soup

This classic vegetarian soup, better known as pistou, is rich in colour and flavour.

ingredients

SERVES FOUR TO SIX

- 150g/5oz/scant 1 cup dried haricot (navy) beans, soaked overnight in cold water
- 150g/5oz/scant 1 cup dried flageolet or cannellini beans, soaked overnight in cold water
- 1 onion, chopped
- 1.2 litres/2 pints/5 cups hot vegetable stock
- 2 carrots, roughly chopped
- 225g/8oz Savoy cabbage, shredded
- 1 large potato, about 225g/8oz, roughly chopped
- 225g/8oz French (green) beans, chopped
- 1 bouquet garni
- salt and ground black pepper
- 30ml/2 tbsp ready-made pesto, to serve
- freshly grated Parmesan cheese, to serve
- basil leaves, to garnish

1 Soak a bean pot in cold water for 20 minutes then drain. If you don't have a bean pot use a large casserole dish, but you do not need to soak it. Drain the soaked haricot and flageolet or cannellini beans and place in the bean pot or casserole dish. Add the onion and pour over sufficient cold water to cover the beans. Cover and place the pot in an unheated oven.

2 Preheat the oven to 200°C/400°F/Gas 6 and cook for 1¼ hours.

3 Drain the beans and onions. Place half the beans and onions in a food processor or blender and process to a paste. Return the drained beans and the bean paste to the bean pot or casserole. Add the hot vegetable stock and stir well.

4 Add the carrots, cabbage, potato and French beans to the pot. Season with salt and pepper, cover and return to the oven. Reduce the oven temperature to 180°C/350°F/Gas 4 and cook for 1 hour, or until the vegetables are cooked.

5 Remove the pot from the oven and stir in half of the pesto. Stir in the grated Parmesan cheese. Ladle the soup into warmed soup bowls. Top each bowl of soup with a teaspoon of the remaining pesto and serve garnished with fresh basil.

NUTRITIONAL INFORMATION: Energy 338kcal/1416kJ; Protein 17.2g; Carbohydrate 34.6g, of which sugars 7.5g; Fat 15.5g, of which saturates 3.8g; Cholesterol 10mg; Calcium 215mg; Fibre 10.8g; Sodium 133mg.

Pea & Barley Soup

This hearty, traditional soup makes a meal in itself on a cold winter's day.

ingredients

SERVES SIX

- 225g/8oz/1¼ cups yellow split peas
- 25g/1oz/¼ pearl barley
- 1.75 litres/3 pints/7½ cups vegetable or ham stock
- 50g/2oz smoked streaky (fatty) bacon, cubed
- 25g/1oz/2 tbsp butter
- 1 onion, finely chopped
- 2 garlic cloves, crushed
- 225g/8oz celeriac, cubed
- 15ml/1 tbsp chopped fresh marjoram
- salt and ground black pepper
- crusty bread, to serve

1 Rinse the peas and barley in cold water. Put in a bowl, cover with water and soak overnight.

2 The next day, drain and rinse the pulses. Put them in a large pan, pour in the stock and bring to the boil. Simmer gently for 40 minutes.

3 Dry fry the bacon cubes in a frying pan for 5 minutes, or until well browned and crispy. Remove with a slotted spoon, leaving the fat behind and set aside.

4 Add the butter to the frying pan, add the onion and garlic and cook gently for 5 minutes. Add the celeriac and cook for a further 5 mintues, or until the onion is just starting to colour.

5 Add the softenened vegetables and bacon to the pan of stock, peas and barley.

6 Season with salt and pepper, then cover and simmer for 20 minutes, or until the soup is thick. Stir in the marjoram, add extra black pepper to taste and serve piping hot.

cook's tip

If you like, add croûtons to the soup by spreading cut bread with herb or garlic butter before baking in the oven. Alternatively, you could sprinkle slices of bread with freshly grated Parmesan cheese and bake until the cheese is golden and bubbling. Add to the soup when served.

NUTRITIONAL INFORMATION: Energy 195kcal/820kJ; Protein 10.9g; Carbohydrate 25.8g, of which sugars 1.8g; Fat 6.1g, of which saturates 2.9g; Cholesterol 14mg; Calcium 39mg; Fibre 2.4g; Sodium 167mg.

Haddock & Potato Soup

This creamy, traditional Scottish soup is made with piquant smoked haddock.

ingredients

SERVES SIX

- 350g/12oz finnan haddock or other undyed smoked haddock
- 1 onion, chopped
- 1 bouquet garni
- 900ml/1½ pints/3¾ cups water
- 500g/1¼lb potatoes, quartered
- 600ml/1 pint/2½ cups milk
- 40g/1½oz/3 tbsp butter
- salt and ground black pepper
- chopped fresh chives, to garnish
- crusty bread, to serve (optional)

1 Put the haddock, onion, bouquet garni and measured water into a large pan and bring to the boil. Skim the scum from the surface, then cover the pan with a tight-fitting lid. Lower the heat and poach gently for 10–15 minutes, or until the haddock flakes easily.

2 Remove the poached fish from the pan using a fish slice and remove the skin and bones. Return these to the pan and simmer, uncovered, for 30 minutes. Meanwhile, flake the flesh and reserve.

3 Strain the fish stock and return to the rinsed-out pan, then add the potatoes and simmer for about 25 minutes, or until tender. Remove the potatoes from the pan using a slotted spoon. Add the milk to the pan and reheat gently.

4 Meanwhile, mash the potatoes with the butter, then whisk into the soup in the pan until thick and creamy. Add the flaked fish to the pan and adjust the seasoning. Ladle into warmed soup bowls, sprinkle with chopped chives and serve immediately with crusty bread, if you like.

cook's tip

Buy traditionally smoked fish, which is quite pale, rather than chemically processed haddock, which is dyed a bright yellow.

NUTRITIONAL INFORMATION: Energy 205kcal/864kJ; Protein 16.1g; Carbohydrate 19g, of which sugars 6.4g; Fat 7.8g, of which saturates 4.7g; Cholesterol 41mg; Calcium 137mg; Fibre 1g; Sodium 132mg.

Leek Terrine & Deli Meats

This attractive appetizer is easy to make but looks spectacular. Cook the terrine a day ahead.

ingredients

SERVES SIX

- 20–24 small young leeks
- about 225g/8oz mixed sliced cooked meats, such as prosciutto, coppa and pancetta
- 50g/2oz/½ cup shelled walnuts, toasted and chopped
- salt and ground black pepper

For the dressing

- 60ml/4 tbsp walnut oil
- 60ml/4 tbsp olive oil
- 30ml/2 tbsp white wine vinegar
- 5ml/1 tsp wholegrain mustard

1 Cut off the roots and most of the green part from the leeks. Wash them thoroughly under cold running water.

2 Bring a large pan of salted water to the boil. Add the leeks, bring the water back to the boil, then simmer for 6–8 minutes, until the leeks are just tender. Drain well.

cook's tip

The terrine is easier to slice when cold, but allow it to come to room temperature to serve.

3 Leave the leeks until they are cool enough to handle, then fill a 450g/1lb loaf tin (pan) with the leeks, placing them alternately head to tail to make even layers, and lightly seasoning each layer as you go with salt and pepper.

4 Put another loaf tin inside the first and gently press down on the leeks. Carefully invert both tins and let any water drain out. Place one or two weights on top of the tins and chill the terrine for at least 4 hours or overnight.

5 To make the dressing, whisk together the walnut and olive oils, vinegar and mustard in a small bowl. Season to taste.

6 Carefully turn out the terrine on to a board and cut into six neat slices using a large, sharp knife. Lay the slices of leek terrine on serving plates and arrange the slices of meat beside them.

7 Spoon the dressing over the slices of terrine and sprinkle with the chopped walnuts. Serve immediately.

NUTRITIONAL INFORMATION: Energy 232kcal/962kJ; Protein 10.5g; Carbohydrate 3.3g, of which sugars 2.6g; Fat 19.7g, of which saturates 2.4g; Cholesterol 22mg; Calcium 37mg; Fibre 2.4g; Sodium 453mg.

Tomato & Cheese Tarts

These crisp little tarts look impressive but are easy to make. They are best eaten fresh from the oven.

ingredients

SERVES FOUR

- 1 egg white
- 2 sheets ready-made filo pastry, thawed if frozen
- 115g/4oz/½ cup low-fat soft (farmer's) cheese
- handful of fresh basil leaves, torn if large
- 3 small tomatoes, thickly sliced
- salt and ground black pepper

variations

- *Substitute crumbled goat's cheese or feta for the soft (farmer's) cheese or cut a goat's cheese log into eight slices.*

- *Top the tomato slices with a few pieces of chopped anchovy and a pitted black olive. Omit the salt from the seasoning.*

- *Use four red and four yellow cherry tomatoes, halved and in two-colour pairs, to decorate the tops of these tartlets.*

- *Sprinkle the tartlets with chopped fresh chives when they have been assembled.*

cook's tip

Filo pastry can be made at home but the process is quite laborious and takes a long time. It is much easier to buy chilled or frozen ready-made dough, which is readily available in delicatessens and supermarkets.

The sheets dry out very quickly: don't open the packet until you start to work on the pastry, and keep the pile of sheets covered with a damp cloth. Brushing with melted butter, oil or egg white before baking keeps the pastry flexible while you shape it and makes sure that the layers are crisp when cooked. There is no need to grease the tins.

1 Preheat the oven to 200°C/400°F/Gas 5. Beat the egg white lightly with a fork, just to break it up.

2 Brush the sheets of filo pastry lightly with egg white and, using a sharp knife, cut into sixteen 10cm/4in squares.

3 Layer the filo squares in pairs in eight patty tins (muffin pans). Spoon the cheese into the pastry cases (pie shells). Season with salt and ground black pepper and top each one with a few basil leaves.

4 Arrange the tomato slices on the tarts, season with salt and pepper and bake for 10–12 minutes, until golden. Serve the tarts warm or at room temperature, garnished with a few small basil leaves.

NUTRITIONAL INFORMATION: Energy 118kcal/497kJ; Protein 7.3g; Carbohydrate 17.9g, of which sugars 3.6g; Fat 2.8g, of which saturates 1.6g; Cholesterol 7mg; Calcium 65mg; Fibre 1.3g; Sodium 149mg.

Pears with Stilton

Firm juicy pears and piquant cheese are a truly magical combination in this classic appetizer.

ingredients

SERVES FOUR

- 4 ripe pears
- 75g/3oz blue Stilton cheese
- 50g/2oz/3 tbsp curd (farmer's) cheese
- mixed salad leaves
- salt and ground black pepper
- walnut halves and sprigs of fresh parsley, to garnish

For the dressing

- 45ml/3 tbsp light olive oil
- 15ml/1 tbsp lemon juice
- 10ml/2 tsp toasted poppy seeds

variations

· Stilton is the usual cheese used in this classic dish but you could also use Roquefort or Gorgonzola.

· Another old British dish combining pears with Stilton is Locket's Savoury, traditionally served at the end of a meal but also good as a first course: toast slices of crustless white bread, cover with watercress and sliced pears, top with slivers of Stilton and bake at 200°/400°/Gas 6 for 5–10 minutes until the cheese is melted and bubbling.

1 First make the dressing. Place the olive oil, lemon juice and poppy seeds in a screw-topped jar and season with salt and pepper. Close the lid and shake well until combined.

2 Cut the pears in half lengthways, then scoop out the cores and cut away the calyx from the rounded end.

cook's tip

The pears should be lightly chilled in the refrigerator before they are used in this dish.

3 Crumble the Stilton into a bowl and beat it together with the curd cheese and a little pepper. Divide this mixture among the cavities in the pears, spooning it into mounds. Arrange the salad leaves onto plates and add the pears.

4 Shake the dressing to mix it again, then spoon it over the pears. Serve garnished with walnut halves and parsley.

NUTRITIONAL INFORMATION: Energy 243kcal/1007kJ; Protein 7.2g; Carbohydrate 15.5g, of which sugars 15.5g; Fat 17.2g, of which saturates 6.4g; Cholesterol 21mg; Calcium 109mg; Fibre 3.5g; Sodium 208mg.

Smoked Haddock Pâté

This pâté is best made with Arbroath Smokies, small haddock that are salted and hot-smoked.

ingredients

SERVES SIX

- butter, for greasing
- 3 large Arbroath Smokies (about 225g/8oz each) or other undyed smoked haddock
- 275g/10oz/1¼ cups medium-fat soft (farmer's) cheese
- 3 eggs, lightly beaten
- 30–45ml/2–3 tbsp lemon juice
- freshly ground black pepper
- sprigs of fresh chervil, to garnish
- lemon wedges and lettuce leaves, to serve

1 Preheat the oven to 160°C/325°F/Gas 3. Generously grease six individual ramekins with butter.

2 Place the fish in an ovenproof dish and heat through in the oven for 10 minutes. Remove and discard the skin and bones, then flake the flesh into a bowl.

3 Mash the fish with a fork and gradually work in the cheese, then the eggs. Add the lemon juice and season with black pepper to taste.

4 Divide the fish mixture among the six ramekins and place in a roasting pan. Pour hot water into the roasting pan to come about halfway up the sides of the dishes. Bake the pâté for 30 minutes, until it is just set.

5 Leave to cool for 2–3 minutes, then run a knife point around the edge of each dish and invert on to a warmed plate. Garnish with fresh chervil sprigs and serve immediately with the lemon wedges and lettuce leaves.

variations

• *This pâté is also tasty made with hot-smoked trout fillets. You can then omit the initial cooking of the fish in step 2.*

• *Leave the pâté to cool and serve with a salad.*

NUTRITIONAL INFORMATION: Energy 253kcal/1049kJ; Protein 17.9g; Carbohydrate 1.4g, of which sugars 1.4g; Fat 19.6g, of which saturates 6.6g; Cholesterol 151mg; Calcium 46mg; Fibre 0g; Sodium 527mg.

Egg, Tomato & Crab Salad

You could adjust the quantities in this tasty salad to make a quick, light and healthy lunch dish.

ingredients

SERVES FOUR

- 1 round (butterhead) lettuce
- 2 x 200g/7oz cans crab meat, drained
- 4 hard-boiled eggs, sliced
- 16 cherry tomatoes, halved
- ½ green (bell) pepper, seeded and thinly sliced
- 6 pitted black olives, sliced

For the dressing

- 45ml/3 tbsp chilli sauce
- 250g/8fl oz/1 cup mayonnaise
- 10ml/2 tsp freshly squeezed lemon juice
- ½ green pepper, seeded and finely chopped
- 5ml/1 tsp prepared horseradish
- 5ml/1 tsp Worcestershire sauce

variations

- *Use freshly cooked crab meat when it is available, or substitute thawed frozen crab meat for canned crab meat.*

- *Substitute well-drained, canned tuna for the crab meat.*

- *Use peeled cooked prawns (shrimp) instead of crab meat, but try to avoid frozen ones as the texture can be woolly.*

- *Make the salad using 16 whole quail's eggs, boiled for 1½ minutes, then cooled and shelled, instead of sliced hard-boiled eggs.*

1 First make the dressing. Place all the ingredients in a bowl and mix well with a balloon whisk. Cover the bowl with clear film (plastic wrap) and set aside in a cool place until required.

2 Line four plates with the lettuce leaves. Break up the crab meat with a fork and divide it among the plates, mounding it up in the centre of each plate.

3 Arrange the slices of egg around the outside of the crab meat, with the tomato halves on top of them.

4 Spoon a little of the dressing over the crab meat. Arrange the green pepper slices on top and sprinkle with the olives. Serve immediately with the remaining dressing handed separately.

cook's tip

Check through the crab meat before adding it to the salad to make sure it does not contain any pieces of shell.

NUTRITIONAL INFORMATION: Energy 608kcal/2515kJ; Protein 25.9g; Carbohydrate 4.8g, of which sugars 4.5g; Fat 54.2g, of which saturates 9g; Cholesterol 309mg; Calcium 171mg; Fibre 1.3g; Sodium 1018mg.

Spinach & Prawn Salad

Serve this warm salad with plenty of crusty bread to mop up the delicious juices.

ingredients

SERVES FOUR

- 105ml/7 tbsp olive oil
- 30ml/2 tbsp sherry vinegar
- 2 garlic cloves, peeled and finely chopped
- 5ml/1 tsp Dijon mustard
- 12 cooked king prawns (jumbo shrimp), in the shell
- 115g/4oz rindless streaky (fatty) bacon, cut into small strips
- 115g/4oz/2 cups fresh young spinach leaves
- ½ head oak leaf lettuce, coarsely torn
- salt and ground black pepper

1 To make the dressing, whisk together 90ml/6 tbsp of the olive oil with the vinegar, garlic and mustard in a small pan and season to taste with salt and pepper. Heat gently, whisking constantly, until slightly thickened, then remove from the heat and keep warm while you make the salad.

2 Remove the heads and peel the prawns, leaving their tails intact. Cut along the back of each prawn and remove the dark vein. Set the prawns aside until needed.

3 Heat the remaining olive oil in a frying pan over medium heat. Add the strips of bacon and cook, stirring occasionally, until they are golden and crisp. Add the prawns and stir-fry for a few minutes until just warmed through.

4 Meanwhile, arrange the spinach leaves with the oak leaf lettuce leaves on four individual serving plates.

5 Spoon the bacon and prawns on to the leaves, then pour the hot dressing over them. Serve the salad immediately.

cook's tip

Sherry vinegar lends a pungent, nutty flavour to this delicious salad, but ordinary red or white wine vinegar could be used instead if you like.

NUTRITIONAL INFORMATION: Energy 320kcal/1325kJ; Protein 18.8g; Carbohydrate 0.9g, of which sugars 0.9g; Fat 26.8g, of which saturates 5.3g; Cholesterol 165mg; Calcium 117mg; Fibre 0.8g; Sodium 546mg.

Smoked Trout Salad

Horseradish goes beautifully with smoked trout and combines with yogurt to make a lovely dressing.

ingredients

SERVES FOUR

- 1 oak leaf or other dark-coloured lettuce, such as lollo rosso
- 225g/8oz small ripe tomatoes, cut into thin wedges
- ½ cucumber, peeled and thinly sliced
- 4 smoked trout fillets, about 200g/7oz each, skinned and coarsely flaked

For the dressing

- pinch of English (hot) mustard powder, or 2.5ml/½tsp prepared English mustard
- 15ml/3 tsp white wine vinegar
- 30ml/2 tbsp light olive oil
- 100ml/3½fl oz/scant ½ cup natural (plain) yogurt
- 30ml/2 tbsp grated fresh or bottled horseradish
- pinch of caster (superfine) sugar

1 To make the dressing, mix together the mustard powder and vinegar in a bowl, then gradually whisk in the olive oil, yogurt, grated horseradish and sugar. Set aside in a cool place for about 30 minutes.

cook's tips

• *There is no need to add salt to the horseradish salad dressing because of the saltiness of the smoked trout fillets.*

• *Look for natural, undyed smoked trout fillets – they should be a delicate cream colour.*

2 Place the lettuce leaves in a large mixing bowl. Whisk the dressing briefly again to amalgamate the ingredients, then pour half of it over the salad and toss lightly using two spoons to coat the leaves evenly in the dressing.

3 Arrange the dressed leaves on four individual plates and add the tomatoes, cucumber and smoked trout.

4 Spoon the remaining dressing over the salads and serve immediately.

NUTRITIONAL INFORMATION: Energy 303kcal/1268kJ; Protein 40.9g; Carbohydrate 4.4g, of which sugars 4.4g; Fat 13.7g, of which saturates 1g; Cholesterol 0mg; Calcium 81mg; Fibre 1g; Sodium 139mg.

Warm Salmon Salad

This light salad is perfect in summer. Serve it as soon as it is ready, or the leaves will lose their colour.

ingredients

SERVES FOUR

- 450g/1lb salmon fillet
- 30ml/2 tbsp sesame oil
- grated rind of ½ orange
- juice of 1 orange
- 5ml/1 tsp Dijon mustard
- 15ml/1 tbsp chopped fresh tarragon
- 45ml/3 tbsp groundnut (peanut) oil
- 115g/4oz fine green beans
- 175g/6oz mixed salad leaves, such as young spinach leaves, radicchio and frisée
- 15ml/1 tbsp toasted sesame seeds
- salt and ground black pepper

1 Skin the salmon fillet, if this has not already been done by your fish supplier, and cut the flesh into bitesize pieces with a sharp knife. Set aside.

2 To make the dressing, mix together the sesame oil, orange rind and juice, mustard and chopped tarragon in a bowl and season to taste with salt and ground black pepper. Set aside.

cook's tip

Choose a fillet from the middle of the fish for even thickness.

3 Heat the groundnut oil in a heavy frying pan over medium heat. Add the pieces of salmon and cook, stirring occasionally, for 3–4 minutes, or until the fish is just lightly browned on the outside but still tender on the inside.

4 Meanwhile, blanch the green beans in a pan of boiling salted water for 5–6 minutes, until tender but still slightly crisp.

5 Add the dressing to the salmon, toss together gently and cook for 30 seconds. Remove the pan from the heat.

6 Arrange the salad leaves on serving plates. Drain the beans and place them over the leaves. Spoon the salmon and its juices over the top, sprinkle with the toasted sesame seeds and serve immediately.

NUTRITIONAL INFORMATION: Energy 362kcal/1499kJ; Protein 24.3g; Carbohydrate 1.7g, of which sugars 1.4g; Fat 28.7g, of which saturates 5g; Cholesterol 56mg; Calcium 72mg; Fibre 1.3g; Sodium 53mg.

Fried Plaice

This simple dish is very popular with children and makes an excellent light lunch or supper.

ingredients

SERVES FOUR

- 25g/1oz/½ cup plain flour
- 2 eggs, beaten
- 75g/3oz/1½ cup dried breadcrumbs
- 4 small plaice, black skin removed
- 15g/½oz/1 tbsp butter
- 15ml/1 tbsp sunflower oil
- salt and ground black pepper
- fresh basil leaves, to garnish

For the tomato sauce
- 30ml/2 tbsp olive oil
- 1 red onion, finely chopped
- 1 garlic clove, finely chopped
- 400g/14oz can choppped tomatoes
- 15ml/1 tbsp tomato purée (paste)
- 15ml/1 tbsp torn fresh basil leaves

1 First make the tomato sauce. Heat the olive oil in a large pan, add the chopped onion and garlic and cook gently for about 5 minutes, until softened and pale golden. Stir in the chopped tomatoes and tomato purée and simmer for 20–30 minutes, stirring occasionally. Season with salt and pepper and stir in the basil.

2 Spread out the flour in a shallow dish, pour the beaten eggs into another and spread out the breadcrumbs in a third. Season the plaice.

3 Hold a fish in your left hand and dip it first in the plain flour, then in egg and finally in the breadcrumbs, patting the crumbs on with your dry right hand.

4 Heat the butter and oil in a large frying pan until foaming. Fry the fish one at a time in the hot fat for approximately 5 minutes on each side, until golden brown and cooked through, but still juicy in the middle. Drain on kitchen paper and keep hot while you fry the rest of the plaice.

5 Pile the pieces of plaice on to warmed serving plates and serve with lemon wedges and the tomato sauce, garnished with basil leaves.

cook's tip

This recipe works equally well with lemon sole or dabs (these do not need skinning), or fillets of haddock or whiting.

NUTRITIONAL INFORMATION: Energy 323kcal/1354kJ; Protein 20.5g; Carbohydrate 25.4g, of which sugars 5.5g; Fat 16.3g, of which saturates 4.2g; Cholesterol 154mg; Calcium 106mg; Fibre 1.8g; Sodium 338mg.

Spicy Fish Rösti

Serve these delicious fish patties crisp and hot for lunch or supper with a mixed green salad.

ingredients

SERVES FOUR

- 350g/12oz large, firm, waxy potatoes
- 350g/12oz salmon fillet, skinned
- 3–4 spring onions (scallions), finely chopped
- 5ml/1 tsp grated fresh root ginger
- 30ml/2 tbsp chopped fresh coriander (cilantro)
- 10ml/2 tsp lemon juice
- 30ml/2 tbsp sunflower oil
- salt and cayenne pepper
- lemon wedges, to serve
- fresh coriander sprigs, to garnish

1 Scrub the potatoes well but leave their skins on. Bring a large pan of water to the boil, add the potatoes and cook for approximately 10 minutes or until they are just parboiled. Drain the potatoes and plunge into cold water for a few minutes until they are cool enough to handle.

2 Meanwhile, finely chop the salmon and place in a bowl. Stir in the spring onions, ginger, chopped coriander and lemon juice. Season to taste with salt and cayenne pepper.

3 Peel off the skins of the potatoes and grate the flesh coarsely. Add the grated potato to the fish mixture and stir gently until well combined. Form the mixture into 12 patties, pressing the mixture together but leaving the edges slightly uneven so that they will crisp when cooked.

4 Heat the oil in a large frying pan over medium heat. Add the fish rösti, a few at a time, and cook for 3 minutes on each side, until golden brown and crisp. Drain on kitchen paper and keep warm while you cook the remaining rösti. Serve hot with lemon wedges to squeeze over the rosti and garnished with sprigs of fresh coriander.

cook's tip

Do not overcook the potatoes. They need to be quite firm to the touch so that they are easy to grate and do not fall apart.

variation

Make the rösti with white fish or a mixture of 225g/8oz white fish and 115g/4 oz salmon.

NUTRITIONAL INFORMATION: Energy 208kcal/870kJ; Protein 17.7g; Carbohydrate 14.4g, of which sugars 1.4g; Fat 9.2g, of which saturates 1.2g; Cholesterol 40mg; Calcium 17mg; Fibre 1g; Sodium 63mg.

Mediterranean Fish Rolls

Sun-dried tomatoes, pine nuts and anchovies make a flavoursome stuffing for the fish.

ingredients

SERVES FOUR

- 75g/3oz/6 tbsp butter, plus extra for greasing
- 4 plaice or flounder fillets (about 225g/8oz each), skinned
- 1 small onion, chopped
- 1 celery stick, finely chopped
- 115g/4oz/2 cups fresh white breadcrumbs
- 45ml/3 tbsp chopped fresh parsley
- 30ml/2 tbsp pine nuts, toasted
- 3–4 pieces sun-dried tomatoes in oil, drained and chopped
- 50g/2oz can anchovy fillets, drained and chopped
- 75ml/5 tbsp fish stock or water
- ground black pepper

1 Preheat the oven to 180°C/350°F/Gas 4. Grease a shallow, ovenproof dish with butter. Using a sharp knife, cut the fish fillets in half lengthways to make eight smaller fillets and set aside while you make the stuffing.

2 Melt the remaining butter in a heavy pan over low heat. Add the onion and celery, cover the pan with a tight-fitting lid and cook, stirring occasionally, for about 15 minutes, until the vegetables are very soft but not coloured.

3 Mix together the breadcrumbs, parsley, pine nuts, sun-dried tomatoes and anchovies in a bowl. Stir in the softened onion and celery, together with the buttery pan juices, and season the mixture to taste with pepper.

4 Divide the stuffing into eight equal portions. Taking one portion at a time, form the stuffing into a ball then roll it up inside one of the fish fillets. Secure each roll with a wooden cocktail stick (toothpick) and place in the prepared dish.

5 Pour the fish stock or water over the rolls and cover the dish with buttered foil. Bake for about 20 minutes, or until the fish flakes easily with the point of a sharp knife.

6 Remove and discard the cocktail sticks, transfer the rolls to warmed plates, drizzle with a little of the cooking juices and serve immediately.

NUTRITIONAL INFORMATION: Energy 528kcal/2213kJ; Protein 45.9g; Carbohydrate 24.6g, of which sugars 2.8g; Fat 28.1g, of which saturates 11g; Cholesterol 142mg; Calcium 189mg; Fibre 1.3g; Sodium 1100mg.

Mackerel with Spicy Dhal

The oily mackerel is perfectly complemented by tamarind-flavoured lentils in this nutritious dish.

ingredients

SERVES FOUR

- 250g/9oz/1 cup red lentils, or yellow split peas (soaked overnight)
- 1 litre/1¾ pints/4 cups water
- 30ml/2 tbsp sunflower oil
- 2.5ml/½ tsp each mustard seeds, cumin seeds, fennel seeds, and fenugreek or cardamom seeds
- 5ml/1 tsp ground turmeric
- 3–4 dried red chillies, crumbled
- 30ml/1 tbsp tamarind paste
- 5ml/1 tsp soft brown sugar
- 30ml/2 tbsp chopped fresh coriander (cilantro)
- 4 mackerel or 8 large sardines
- salt and ground black pepper
- fresh red chilli slices and finely chopped coriander, to garnish
- flat bread and tomatoes, to serve

1 Rinse the lentils or split peas, drain them thoroughly and put them in a large pan. Lower the heat, partially cover the pan and simmer the pulses for 30–40 minutes, stirring occasionally until they are tender or mushy.

2 Heat the oil in a wok or shallow pan. Add the mustard seeds, then cover and cook for a few seconds, until they pop. Remove the lid, add the rest of the seeds, with the turmeric and chillies and fry for a few more seconds.

3 Stir in the pulses, with salt to taste. Mix well; stir in the tamarind paste and sugar. Bring to the boil, then gently simmer for approximately 10 minutes, until the mixture becomes thick. Stir in the chopped fresh coriander and reserve, keeping the sauce warm.

4 Meanwhile, clean the fish thoroughly then heat a ridged grilling pan or the grill (broiler) until very hot. Make six diagonal slashes on either side of each fish and remove the head and tail if you wish.

5 Season with salt and pepper inside and out, then grill (broil) the fish for 5–7 minutes on each side, until the skin is quite crisp. Serve with the dhal, flat bread and tomatoes, garnished with red chilli and chopped coriander.

NUTRITIONAL INFORMATION: Energy 637kcal/2665kJ; Protein 48.3g; Carbohydrate 36.2g, of which sugars 2.6g; Fat 34.1g, of which saturates 6.6g; Cholesterol 93mg; Calcium 52mg; Fibre 3.1g; Sodium 124mg.

Roast Cod with Pancetta

Served on a bed of butter beans, this makes a superb supper dish.

ingredients

SERVES FOUR

- 200g/7oz/1 cup butter (lima) beans, soaked overnight in cold water to cover
- 2 leeks, thinly sliced
- 2 garlic cloves, chopped
- 8 fresh sage leaves
- 90ml/6 tbsp fruity olive oil
- 8 thin slices of pancetta
- 4 thick cod steaks, skinned
- 12 cherry tomatoes
- salt and ground black pepper
- flat-leat parsley, to garnish

1 Drain the butter beans, tip into a large pan and cover with cold water. Bring to the boil and skim off the foam on the surface. Lower the heat, then stir in the leeks, garlic, four sage leaves and 30ml/ 2 tbsp of the olive oil.

2 Simmer for approximately 1–1½ hours, or until the beans are tender, adding more water if necessary. Drain away the excess liquid, return to the pan, season with salt and pepper, stir in 30ml/2 tbsp olive oil and keep warm.

3 Preheat the oven to 200°C/400°F/Gas 6. Wrap two slices of pancetta around the edge of each cod steak, tying it on with kitchen string or securing it with a wooden cocktail stick (toothpick). Insert a sage leaf between the pancetta and the cod. Season the fish with salt and pepper.

variation

You can use cannellini beans for this recipe, and streaky (fatty) bacon instead of pancetta. It is also good made with halibut, hake, haddock or salmon.

4 Heat a heavy frying pan, add 15ml/1 tbsp of the remaining oil and seal the cod steaks two at a time for 1 minute on each side. Transfer them to an ovenproof dish and roast in the oven for 5 minutes.

5 Add the tomatoes to the dish and drizzle over the remaining olive oil. Roast for 5 minutes more, until the cod steaks are cooked but still juicy. Serve them on a bed of butter beans with the roasted tomatoes. Garnish with chopped flat-leaf parsley.

NUTRITIONAL INFORMATION: Energy 449kcal/1883kJ; Protein 44.5g; Carbohydrate 25.3g, of which sugars 3.9g; Fat 19.5g, of which saturates 3g; Cholesterol 84mg; Calcium 85mg; Fibre 9.8g; Sodium 403mg.

Fish and Shellfish Stew

If any mussels fail to open when cooked they should be discarded.

ingredients

SERVES FOUR

- 225g/8oz/2 cups cooked prawns (shrimp) in the shell
- 450g/1lb white fish fillets
- 45ml/3 tbsp olive oil
- 1 onion, chopped
- 1 leek, sliced
- 1 carrot, diced
- 1 garlic clove, chopped
- 2.5ml/½ tsp ground turmeric
- 150ml/¼ pint/⅔ cup dry white wine or (hard) cider
- 400g/14oz can chopped tomatoes
- 1 sprig each of fresh parsley, thyme and fennel
- 1 bay leaf
- small piece of orange rind
- 1 squid, body cut into rings and tentacles chopped
- 12 fresh mussels, scrubbed
- salt and ground black pepper
- 30–45ml/2–3 tbsp fresh Parmesan cheese shavings and fresh parsley, to garnish

For the rouille sauce
- 2 slices white bread, crustless
- 2 garlic cloves, crushed
- ½ fresh red chilli, seeded
- 15ml/1 tbsp tomato purée (paste)
- 45ml/3 tbsp olive oil

1 Remove the heads and peel the prawns, leaving the tails intact. Reserve the shells and devein the prawns. Skin the white fish and cut into bitesize pieces. Make a stock by simmering the shells and fish skins in 450ml/¾ pint/scant 2 cups water for 20 minutes.

2 Heat the oil in a large pan. Add the onion, leek, carrot and garlic and cook, stirring, for 6–7 minutes. Stir in the turmeric and add the wine or cider, tomatoes, strained stock, herbs and orange rind.

3 Bring the mixture to the boil, cover the pan and simmer for 20 minutes.

4 Meanwhile, to make the rouille sauce, process all the sauce ingredients in a food processor or blender.

5 Add the fish and shellfish to the pan. Simmer for 5–6 minutes, until the mussels open.

6 Remove the bay leaf and rind and season to taste. Garnish with Parmesan cheese and parsley. Serve with the rouille.

NUTRITIONAL INFORMATION: Energy 505kcal/2112kJ; Protein 51.7g; Carbohydrate 15.8g, of which sugars 7.8g; Fat 23.8g, of which saturates 5.4g; Cholesterol 349mg; Calcium 252mg; Fibre 3.1g; Sodium 520mg.

Fish Pie

This traditional dish uses a combination of fresh and smoked fish for a well-rounded flavour.

ingredients

SERVES FOUR

- 450g/1lb fresh haddock or cod fillet
- 225g/8oz smoked haddock or cod fillet
- 150ml/¼ pint/⅔ cup skimmed milk
- 150ml/¼ pint/⅔ cup water
- 1 slice of lemon
- 1 small bay leaf
- a few fresh parsley stalks
- 450g/1lb potatoes, boiled and mashed
- 25g/1oz/2 tbsp butter

For the sauce

- 25g/1oz/2 tbsp butter
- 25g/1oz/¼ cup plain (all-purpose) flour
- 5ml/1 tsp lemon juice, or to taste
- 45ml/3 tbsp chopped fresh parsley
- ground black pepper

1 Preheat the oven to 190°C/375°F/Gas 5. Put the fish into a pan with the milk, water, lemon, bay leaf and parsley stalks. Heat slowly until bubbles are rising to the surface, then cover and simmer gently for about 10 minutes until the fish is cooked.

2 Lift out the fish, then strain and reserve 300ml/½ pint/1¼ cups of the cooking liquor. Leave the fish until cool enough to handle, then flake the flesh and discard the skin and bones. Set aside.

3 To make the sauce, melt the butter in a pan, add the flour and cook for 1–2 minutes over low heat, stirring constantly. Gradually add the reserved cooking liquor, stirring well until smooth. Simmer gently, stirring, for 1–2 minutes. Remove from the heat and stir in the fish, parsley and lemon juice. Season to taste with black pepper.

variation

Cooked shellfish, such as mussels and prawns (shrimp), can be added to the filling.

4 Turn the fish mixture into a buttered 1.75 litre/3 pint/7½ cup ovenproof dish. Top with the mashed potato, either piping it or spooning it over and roughening the surface with a fork. Dot with butter and bake for about 20 minutes, until heated through and golden brown on top.

NUTRITIONAL INFORMATION: Energy 336kcal/1413kJ; Protein 35.1g; Carbohydrate 24.3g, of which sugars .9g; Fat 11.6g, of which saturates 6.7g; Cholesterol 87mg; Calcium 45mg; Fibre 1.7g; Sodium 587mg.

Fishcakes

Home-made fishcakes are an underrated dish, bearing little resemblance to the store-bought type.

ingredients

SERVES FOUR

- 450g/1lb mixed white and smoked fish fillets, such as haddock or cod, or fresh salmon fillet
- 450g/1lb cooked, mashed potatoes
- 25g/1oz/2 tbsp butter, diced
- 45ml/3 tbsp chopped fresh parsley
- 1 egg, separated
- 1 egg, beaten
- about 50g/2oz/1 cup fine white breadcrumbs made with day-old bread
- salt and ground black pepper
- vegetable oil, for frying

1 Place the fresh and smoked fish in a large pan, season with salt and pepper and pour in water just to cover. Bring to the boil, then lower the heat, cover and simmer for about 10 minutes, until the flesh flakes easily with the tip of a knife. Remove the fish with a slotted spatula and leave until cool enough to handle. Discard the cooking liquid.

cook's tip

You could keep the cooking liquid to use as a fish stock.

2 Remove and discard the skin and any bones from the fish, then flake the flesh. Place the potatoes in a bowl and beat in the fish, butter, parsley and egg yolk. Season the mixture to taste with pepper (and salt if you are not using smoked fish).

3 Divide the fish mixture into eight equal portions, then, with floured hands, form each portion into a flat patty.

4 Beat the remaining egg white with the whole egg. Dip each fishcake into the beaten egg, then turn it carefully in the breadcrumbs to coat evenly.

5 Heat the oil in a frying pan over a medium heat. Add the fishcakes and cook for 3–5 minutes on each side, until crisp and golden. Serve immediately.

NUTRITIONAL INFORMATION: Energy 399kcal/1670kJ; Protein 27.5g; Carbohydrate 28.2g, of which sugars 2.1g; Fat 20.4g, of which saturates 5.6g; Cholesterol 160mg; Calcium 71mg; Fibre 2g; Sodium 252mg.

Salmon with Spicy Pesto

This pesto is made with chilli and sunflower seeds instead of the classic basil and pine nuts.

1 Insert a sharp knife near the top of the salmon's backbone. Working closely to the bone, cut to the end of the steak so one side of it is released from the bone. Repeat with the other side. Pull out any extra visible bones with a pair of tweezers.

2 Holding one end of the salmon, skinside down, insert a small sharp knife under the skin and, working away from you, cut off the skin, keeping as close to the skin as possible. Repeat with the three remaining pieces of fish.

3 Rub the sunflower oil into the fish rounds and place in a non-metallic dish. Add the lime juice and rind, cover the dish with clear film (plastic wrap) and place in the refrigerator to marinate for 2 hours.

4 To make the pesto, put the chillies, garlic, seeds, lime rind and juice in a food processor or blender and season with salt and pepper. Process until well mixed. With the motor running, gradually pour in the olive oil until the sauce has thickened and emulsified.

5 Preheat the grill (broiler). Drain the salmon from its marinade. Grill the fish steaks for about 5 minutes on each side, until the fish is opaque and flakes with the point of a knife. Serve immediately with the spicy pesto.

cook's tip

Try to remove all pieces of fish bone from the fillets. Salmon fish bones are very fine but it is possible to feel any that remain by sliding your forefinger along the length of the fillet against the natural fall of the flesh.

NUTRITIONAL INFORMATION: Energy 653kcal/2719kJ; Protein 50.5g; Carbohydrate 1.4g, of which sugars 0.1g; Fat 49.6g, of which saturates 7.5g; Cholesterol 122mg; Calcium 60mg; Fibre 0.5g; Sodium 111mg.

Pan-fried Garlic Sardines

A garnish of lightly fried sliced garlic cloves goes well with the strong flavour of the fish.

ingredients

SERVES FOUR
- 1.2kg/2½lb fresh sardines
- 30ml/2 tbsp olive oil
- 4 garlic cloves
- finely grated rind of 2 lemons
- 30ml/2 tbsp chopped fresh parsley
- salt and ground black pepper

For the tomato bread
- 8 slices crusty bread, toasted
- 2 large ripe beefsteak tomatoes

variation

This dish could also be made with sprats or fresh anchovies when they are available.

1 First, scale the sardines. Hold each fish by the tail under cold running water and run your other hand from tail to head to scrape off the scales. Cut off the head if you like. Slit open the belly, using a sharp knife, and remove the guts with your fingers. Rinse the body cavity well under cold running water and pat dry with kitchen paper.

2 Heat the olive oil in a heavy frying pan over medium-low heat. Add the garlic cloves and cook, stirring frequently, for 1–2 minutes, until soft.

3 Push the garlic to the side of the pan and add the sardines. Cook, turning once, for 4–5 minutes until light golden brown. Sprinkle the lemon rind and parsley over the fish and season to taste with salt and black pepper.

4 Cut the tomatoes in half and rub them on to the toast. Discard the skins. Serve the sardines with the tomato toast.

cook's tips

· *Scaling the sardines is, without question, a very messy and time-consuming business. However, the fish are so much nicer to eat when scaled that it is worth the effort. (Clear the discarded scales from the sink afterwards.)*

· *Make sure you use very ripe beefsteak tomatoes to make this dish so they will rub on to the toast easily.*

NUTRITIONAL INFORMATION: Energy 513kcal/2149kJ; Protein 47.4g; Carbohydrate 27.9g, of which sugars 4.5g; Fat 24.1g, of which saturates 5.8g; Cholesterol 0mg; Calcium 279mg; Fibre 2g; Sodium 504mg.

Red Mullet with Oranges

This delicately flavoured fish is beautifully complemented by the tangy aroma of orange.

ingredients

SERVES FOUR

- a few sprigs of fresh dill
- 4 large red mullet, total weight 1–1.2kg/2¼–2½lb, gutted and cleaned
- 2 large oranges, halved
- ½ lemon
- 60ml/4 tbsp extra virgin olive oil
- 30ml/2 tbsp pine nuts
- salt
- roasted potatoes, to serve
- green salad leaves, to serve

variation

If you prefer, you can use other herbs to flavour the fish. Basil, rosemary or thyme would all work equally well.

1 Place some fresh dill in the cavity of each fish and lay them in a baking dish, preferably one that can be taken straight to the table.

2 Set half an orange aside and squeeze the rest, along with the lemon. Mix the juice with the olive oil, then pour the mixture over the fish. Turn the fish so that they are evenly coated in the marinade, then cover and leave in a cool place to marinate for 1–2 hours, spooning the marinade over the fish occasionally.

3 Preheat the oven to 180°C/350°F/Gas 4. Sprinkle a little salt over each fish. Slice the reserved half orange into thin rounds, then cut each round into quarters. Place three orange wedges over each fish.

cook's tip

Other fish with fine-flavoured flesh may also be cooked this way. These include sea bass, sea bream, porgy and goa fish. Whichever fish you use, it's best to trim the fins, and this is essential with those that have sharp spines.

4 Bake for 20 minutes, then remove the dish from the oven, baste the fish with the juices and sprinkle the pine nuts over the top. Return the dish to the oven and bake for a further 10–15 minutes. Test the thickest fish to make sure that it is cooked through thoroughly. Place on warmed dinner plates and pour over the remaining juices from the pan. Serve with roast potatoes and a green salad.

NUTRITIONAL INFORMATION: Energy 344kcal/1434kJ; Protein 30.5g; Carbohydrate 5.4g, of which sugars 5.4g; Fat 22.5g, of which saturates 1.9g; Cholesterol 0mg; Calcium 137mg; Fibre 1.2g; Sodium 153mg.

Middle Eastern Sea Bream

The fish is baked on a bed of rice fragrant with herbs and spices and studded with nuts and fruit.

ingredients

SERVES FOUR

- 1.75kg/4lb sea bream or porgy or 2 or 4 smaller sea bream or porgy
- 30ml/2 tbsp olive oil
- 75g/3oz/¾ cup pine nuts
- 1 large onion, finely chopped
- 450g/1lb ripe tomatoes, coarsely chopped
- 75g/3oz/½ cup raisins
- 2.5ml/½ tsp ground cinnamon
- 2.5ml/½ tsp mixed (apple pie) spice
- 45ml/3 tbsp chopped fresh mint
- 225g/8oz/generous 1 cup long grain rice
- 3 lemon slices
- 300ml/½ pint/1¼ cups fish stock

1 Trim the fins, scale the fish, then gut or ask your fish supplier to do this for you. Rinse the fish well under cold running water and pat dry with kitchen paper. Meanwhile, preheat the oven to 175°C/350°F/Gas 4.

2 Heat the oil in a large, heavy pan over medium-low heat. Add the pine nuts and stir-fry for 1 minute until lightly browned. Add the onion and continue to stir-fry until it is softened but not coloured. Add the tomatoes and simmer for 10 minutes.

3 Stir in the raisins, half the cinnamon, half the mixed spice and the mint. Add the rice and lemon slices and stir to coat the rice in the oil.

cook's tips

• If you want to serve one fish per person, buy the smallest fish you can find, weighing about 450g/1lb each, and arrange in a single layer on the rice.

• If you prefer, replace the pine nuts with the same quantity of blanched almonds and split them in half before stir-frying.

4 Transfer the mixture to a large roasting pan and pour the fish stock over the top.

5 Place the fish on top and cut several slashes in the skin. Sprinkle over a little salt, with the remaining mixed spice and cinnamon. Bake for 30–35 minutes for a large fish or 20–25 minutes for smaller fish, until the fish is opaque and the rice tender.

NUTRITIONAL INFORMATION: Energy 562kcal/2348kJ; Protein 39.7g; Carbohydrate 46g, of which sugars 1.1g; Fat 24.1g, of which saturates 1.7g; Cholesterol 71mg; Calcium 89mg; Fibre 0.5g; Sodium 208mg.

Fish in Spicy Sauce

The tasty tomato and herb sauce perfectly complements this easy fish dish.

ingredients

SERVES FOUR TO SIX

- 300ml/½ pint/1¼ cups passata
- 150ml/¼ pint/⅔ cup fish stock
- 1 large onion, finely chopped
- 60ml/4 tbsp chopped fresh coriander (cilantro) leaves
- 60ml/4 tbsp chopped fresh parsley
- 5–8 garlic cloves, crushed
- chopped fresh chilli or chilli paste, to taste
- large pinch of ground ginger
- large pinch of curry powder
- 1.5ml/¼ tsp ground cumin
- 1.5ml/¼ tsp ground turmeric
- seeds from 2–3 cardamom pods
- juice of 2 lemons, plus extra if needed
- 30ml/2 tbsp vegetable or olive oil
- 1.5kg/3¼lb mixed white fish fillets
- salt and ground black pepper
- green vegetables, to serve

1 Put the passata, stock, onion, herbs, garlic, chilli, ginger, curry powder, cumin, turmeric, cardamom, lemon juice and oil in a large pan and bring to the boil.

2 Remove the pan from the heat and add the fish fillets to the hot sauce. Return to the heat and allow the sauce to boil briefly again. Reduce the heat and simmer gently for about 5 minutes, or until the fish is tender. (Test the fish with a fork. If the flesh flakes easily, then it is cooked.)

3 Taste the sauce and adjust the seasoning, adding more lemon juice if necessary. Serve warm with steamed vegetables, if you like.

Variation

- *This dish is just as good using only one type of fish such as cod or flounder.*

- *Instead of poaching the fish, wrap each piece in ready made puff pastry and bake at 190°C/375°F/Gas 5 for about 20 minutes, then serve with the tomato sauce.*

NUTRITIONAL INFORMATION: Energy 191kcal/803kJ; Protein 35.1g; Carbohydrate 3.3g, of which sugars 2.7g; Fat 4.2g, of which saturates 0.5g; Cholesterol 86mg; Calcium 39mg; Fibre 0.9g; Sodium 202mg.

Garlic Chilli Prawns

In Spain gambas al ajillo are cooked in small earthenware dishes, but a frying pan works just as well.

ingredients

SERVES FOUR

- 60ml/4 tbsp olive oil
- 2–3 garlic cloves, finely chopped
- ½ –1 fresh red chilli, seeded and chopped
- 5ml/1 tsp cumin seeds
- 16 cooked Mediterranean prawns (large shrimp)
- 15ml/1 tbsp fresh coriander (cilantro)
- salt and ground black pepper
- lemon wedges and French bread, to serve

3 Add the coriander to the pan, remove from the heat and place four prawns in each of four warmed bowls. Spoon the flavoured oil over them. Serve with lemon wedges for squeezing and French bread to mop up the juices.

Cook's tip

Raw prawns must be deveined before cooking. Pull off the head and legs, then peel off the body shell with your fingers. Leave on the tail fan if you wish. Make a shallow incision down the centre of the back, cutting all the way from the tail to the head. Pick out the thin black vein that runs the length of the prawn with the tip of the knife and discard.

1 Heat the olive oil in a frying pan over medium heat. Add the chopped garlic, cumin seeds and chilli and fry, stirring constantly, for 1 minute, until the garlic softens and just begins to turn brown, but do not allow it to burn.

2 Add the prawns and stir-fry for 3–4 minutes, coating them well with the flavoured oil.

Variation

Use raw prawns (shrimp), and stir-fry for 5–6 minutes until pink.

NUTRITIONAL INFORMATION: Energy 157kcal/653kJ; Protein 13.3g; Carbohydrate 0.1g, of which sugars 0.1g; Fat 11.5g, of which saturates 1.7g; Cholesterol 146mg; Calcium 67mg; Fibre 0.2g; Sodium 144mg.

Spaghetti Marinara

The traditional tomato-based seafood sauce in this dish is popular in Italy's coastal regions.

ingredients

SERVES FOUR

- 30ml/2 tbsp olive oil
- 1 onion, chopped
- 1 garlic clove, finely chopped
- 2 large ripe tomatoes
- 750ml/1¼ pints/3 cups fish stock
- 1kg/2¼ lb clams, cleaned
- 120ml/4fl oz/½ cup anis spirit, such as Ricard or Pernod
- 120ml/4fl oz/½ cup dry white wine
- juice of ¼ lemon
- 300g/11oz spaghetti, broken into 5cm/2in lengths
- 1 fennel bulb, sliced in thin strips
- 30ml/2 tbsp chopped parsley
- salt and ground black pepper
- fennel fronds or fresh dill, to garnish

1 Heat the olive oil in a casserole big enough to contain all the ingredients. Fry the onion gently until soft. Add the garlic.

2 Put the tomatoes in a bowl, pour over boiling water and leave for 10 minutes. Rinse the tomatoes under cold water to cool slightly and then peel the tomatoes, discarding the skins. Chop the flesh, add to the casserole and strain in the tomato juices into the pan. Cook until reduced to a pulp, then add 250ml/8fl oz/ 1 cup of the stock.

3 Discard any open or cracked clams. Add the rest to the pan in three batches. As they open, remove most from the shells and transfer to a plate. Discard any clams that remain shut.

4 Add the anis spirit and white wine to the sauce, plus the remaining fish stock and lemon juice, to taste. Add the pasta and sliced fennel. Season and simmer, partially covered, for 10 minutes. Stir every now and then to separate the strands, and to make sure the pasta is not sticking.

5 When the pasta is cooked, stir in the parsley and check the seasoning. Scatter the clams across the top and cover tightly. Leave to stand for about 10 minutes or so or until the clams warm through and the liquid is absorbed. Serve in bowls, sprinkled with the fennel fronds.

NUTRITIONAL INFORMATION: Energy 331kcal/1394kJ; Protein 15.1g; Carbohydrate 43.6g, of which sugars 6.1g; Fat 5.1g, of which saturates 0.8g; Cholesterol 34mg; Calcium 73mg; Fibre 3.2g; Sodium 610mg.

Seafood Paella

Use monkfish instead of cod, if you like, and add a red mullet or snapper cut into chunks.

ingredients

SERVES FOUR

- 60ml/4 tbsp olive oil
- 225g/8oz cod fillet, skinned and cut into chunks
- 3 prepared baby squid, bodies cut into rings and tentacles chopped into short lengths
- 1 onion, chopped
- 3 garlic cloves, finely chopped
- 1 red (bell) pepper, seeded and sliced
- 4 tomatoes, peeled and chopped
- 225g/8oz/1¼ cups Valencia or risotto rice
- 450ml/¾ pint/scant 2 cups fish stock
- 150ml/¼ pint/⅔ cup dry white wine
- 75g/3oz/¼ cup frozen peas
- 4–5 saffron threads, soaked for about 30 minutes in 30ml/2 tbsp hot water
- 115g/4oz/1 cup cooked peeled prawns (shrimp)
- 8 fresh mussels, scrubbed and debearded
- 10 medium clams, scrubbed
- salt and ground black pepper
- 15ml/1 tbsp chopped fresh parsley, to garnish

1 Heat 30ml/2 tbsp of the olive oil in a heavy frying pan over medium heat. Add the cod and squid and stir-fry for 2 minutes. Transfer to a bowl.

2 Heat the remaining oil in the pan over low heat. Add the onion, garlic and red pepper and cook, stirring occasionally, for 6–7 minutes, until softened but not coloured. Stir in the tomatoes and cook for a further 2 minutes, then add the rice, stirring to coat the grains with oil, and cook for 2–3 minutes more.

3 Pour in the fish stock and wine and add the peas and saffron with its soaking water. Season with salt and pepper.

4 Gently stir in the reserved cooked fish with all the juices, followed by the prawns. Push the mussels and clams into the rice. Cover with a tight-fitting lid and cook over low heat for about 30 minutes. Remove from the heat, keep covered and leave to stand for 5 minutes. Discard any mussels or clams that have not opened. Sprinkle with parsley and serve.

NUTRITIONAL INFORMATION: Energy 478kcal/1998kJ; Protein 29.8g; Carbohydrate 53.1g, of which sugars 6.9g; Fat 13.4g, of which saturates 2g; Cholesterol 198mg; Calcium 74mg; Fibre 2.1g; Sodium 181mg.

Chicken with Celeriac

A stuffing of celeriac and brown breadcrumbs gives roast chicken an unusual and delicious twist.

ingredients

SERVES FOUR

- 1.6kg/3½lb chicken
- 15g/½oz/1 tbsp butter

For the stuffing

- 450g/1lb celeriac, peeled and cut into chunks
- 25g/1oz/2 tbsp butter
- 3 rashers (strips) bacon, chopped
- 2 garlic cloves, finely chopped
- leaves from 1 fresh thyme sprig, chopped
- leaves from 1 small fresh tarragon sprig, chopped
- 30ml/2 tbsp chopped fresh parsley
- 75g/3oz/1½ cups fresh brown breadcrumbs
- dash of Worcestershire sauce
- 1 egg, beaten
- salt and ground black pepper

1 To make the stuffing, cook the celeriac in a pan of boiling water until tender. Drain well and chop finely.

2 Melt the butter in a heavy pan over low heat. Add the bacon and garlic and cook, stirring occasionally, for 5–7 minutes, until the garlic is softened but not coloured.

3 Stir in the celeriac, thyme, tarragon and parsley and cook, stirring occasionally, for 2–3 minutes. Preheat the oven to 200°C/400°F/Gas 6.

4 Remove the pan from the heat and stir in the fresh breadcrumbs, Worcestershire sauce and sufficient egg to bind the mixture. Season with salt and pepper. Use this mixture to stuff the neck end of the chicken. Season the chicken all over with salt and pepper and then rub the butter into the skin with your fingertips.

5 Place the chicken in a roasting pan and roast, basting occasionally with the cooking juices, for 1¼–1½ hours, until the juices run clear when the thickest part of the leg is pierced with the point of a sharp knife. Turn off the oven, prop the door open slightly and leave the chicken to rest for about 10 minutes before removing from the oven and carving.

cook's tip

To stop raw celeriac discolouring, drop the pieces as you peel them into water with a squeeze of lemon juice added.

NUTRITIONAL INFORMATION: Energy 507kcal/2116kJ; Protein 43.6g; Carbohydrate 16.8g, of which sugars 2.4g; Fat 30g, of which saturates 11.6g; Cholesterol 233mg; Calcium 99mg; Fibre 1.9g; Sodium 692mg.

Pot-roast Poussin

The French method of cooking these birds keeps them beautifully moist and succulent.

ingredients

SERVES FOUR

- 15ml/1 tbsp olive oil
- 1 onion, sliced
- 1 large garlic clove, sliced
- 50g/2oz/⅓ cup diced smoked bacon
- 2 poussins (about 450g/1lb each)
- 30ml/2 tbsp melted butter
- 2 baby celery hearts, each cut into 4 pieces
- 8 baby carrots
- 2 small courgettes (zucchini), cut into chunks
- 8 small new potatoes
- 600ml/1 pint/2½ cups chicken stock
- 150ml/¼ pint/⅔ cup dry white wine
- 1 bay leaf
- 2 fresh thyme sprigs
- 2 fresh rosemary sprigs
- 15ml/1 tbsp butter, softened
- 15g/½oz/2 tbsp plain (all-purpose) flour
- salt and ground black pepper
- fresh herbs, to garnish

1 Preheat the oven to 190°C/375°F/Gas 5. Heat the oil in a flameproof casserole. Add the onion, garlic and bacon and cook, stirring, for 5–6 minutes until the onion is soft.

2 Brush the poussins with half the melted butter and season with salt and pepper. Add to the casserole with the vegetables. Add the stock, wine and herbs. Cover and bake for 20 minutes. Brush the birds with the remaining melted butter. Bake for a further 25–30 minutes, until golden.

3 Transfer the poussins to a warmed serving platter and cut each in half with poultry shears or scissors. Remove the vegetables with a slotted spoon and arrange around the birds. Cover with foil and keep warm.

4 Remove the herbs from the casserole and discard. Mix the butter and flour to a paste. Bring the cooking liquid to the boil, then whisk in spoonfuls of paste and cook, stirring, to thicken. Season and serve with the poussins and vegetables, garnished with herbs.

cook's tip

A poussin is a young chicken, killed at 4–6 weeks, and is tender and delicately flavoured.

NUTRITIONAL INFORMATION: Energy 549kcal/2290kJ; Protein 30.8g; Carbohydrate 25.8g, of which sugars 7.5g; Fat 34g, of which saturates 12.4g; Cholesterol 163mg; Calcium 76mg; Fibre 3.5g; Sodium 372mg.

Stoved Chicken

The term "stoved" is derived from the French étouffer, meaning to cook in a covered pot.

ingredients

SERVES FOUR

- 1kg/2¼lb potatoes, cut into 5mm/¼in slices
- 2 large onions, thinly sliced
- 15ml/1 tbsp chopped fresh thyme
- 25g/1oz/2 tbsp butter
- 15ml/1 tbsp sunflower oil
- 2 large bacon rashers (strips), chopped
- 4 large chicken portions, halved, or 8 chicken thighs or 8 drumsticks
- 1 bay leaf
- 600ml/1 pint/2½ cups chicken stock
- salt and ground black pepper

1 Preheat the oven to 150°C/300°F/Gas 2. Make a thick layer of half the potato slices in the base of a large, heavy, flameproof casserole, then cover with half the onion. Sprinkle with half the thyme and season the layers with salt and pepper.

cook's tip

If you do not have a very large frying pan, brown the chicken pieces in two batches, pouring off some of the fat from the first batch before adding the second.

2 Heat the butter and oil in a large frying pan over medium heat. Add the bacon and chicken and cook, turning frequently, for 8–10 minutes, until the chicken is browned all over. Using a slotted spoon transfer the chicken and bacon to the casserole. Reserve the fat in the pan.

3 Sprinkle the remaining thyme over the chicken, add the bay leaf and season. Cover with the remaining onion, followed by a neat layer of overlapping potato slices.

4 Pour the stock into the casserole, brush the potatoes with the reserved fat and season again with salt and pepper, then cover the dish with a tight-fitting lid and cook in the oven for about 2 hours, until the chicken is tender.

5 Meanwhile, preheat the grill (broiler). Lift the casserole from the oven and remove the lid. Place under the grill and cook until the slices of potato on the top are beginning to turn golden brown and crisp. Serve immediately.

NUTRITIONAL INFORMATION: Energy 524kcal/2206kJ; Protein 50.9g; Carbohydrate 48.2g, of which sugars 8.9g; Fat 15.5g, of which saturates 6g; Cholesterol 185mg; Calcium 53mg; Fibre 3.3g; Sodium 496mg.

Chicken with Peppers

This colourful and tasty dish comes from the south of Italy, where sweet peppers are plentiful.

ingredients

SERVES FOUR

- 1.5kg/3lb chicken, cut into serving pieces
- 90ml/6 tbsp olive oil
- 2 red onions, thinly sliced
- 2 garlic cloves, finely chopped
- small piece of dried chilli, crumbled (optional)
- 3 large red (bell) peppers, seeded and cut into strips
- 120ml/4fl oz/½ cup dry white wine
- 2 tomatoes, fresh or canned, peeled and chopped
- 45g/3 tbsp chopped fresh parsley
- salt and ground black pepper
- new potatoes, to serve

1 Trim any visible fat off the chicken with a sharp knife and remove excess skin.

2 Heat half the oil in a large heavy pan or flameproof casserole over low heat. Add the onions and cook, stirring occasionally, for 5–7 minutes, until softened but not coloured. Transfer them to a plate.

cook's tip

For a more elegant version of this dish to serve at a dinner party, use boneless chicken breasts.

3 Add the remaining oil to the pan and increase the heat to medium. Add the chicken pieces and cook, turning frequently, for 6–8 minutes, until browned on all sides. Return the onions to the pan and add the garlic and dried chilli, if using.

4 Add the peppers and stir well to coat in the oil. Season to taste with salt and pepper and cook for 3–4 minutes until the peppers begin to soften. Pour in the wine and cook uncovered until the liquid has reduced by about half.

5 Stir in the tomatoes, lower the heat, cover the pan with a tight-fitting lid and cook, stirring occasionally, for 25–30 minutes, until the peppers are soft and the chicken is cooked through. Stir in the parsley and serve with potatoes.

NUTRITIONAL INFORMATION: Energy 512kcal/2127kJ; Protein 31.9g; Carbohydrate 17.2g, of which sugars 15g; Fat 33.3g, of which saturates 8g; Cholesterol 130mg; Calcium 71mg; Fibre 4.4g; Sodium 128mg.

Southern Fried Chicken

Serve this tasty classic American dish with potato wedges for a filling supper with friends.

ingredients

SERVES FOUR

- 15ml/1 tbsp paprika
- 30ml/2 tbsp plain flour
- 4 skinless chicken fillets, each weighing about 175g/6oz
- 30ml/2 tbsp sunflower oil
- salt and ground black pepper
- 150ml/¼ pint/⅔ cup sour cream
- 15ml/1 tbsp snipped chives

For the corn cakes

- 200g/7oz corn kernels
- 350g/12oz mashed potato, cooled
- 25g/1oz/2 tbsp butter

1 Mix the paprika and flour together well on a plate. Coat each chicken breast in the seasoned flour.

2 Heat the oil in a frying pan and add the chicken breasts. Cook over a high heat until a golden brown colour all over.

cook's tip

To make the mashed potato, cook the potatoes in boiling salted water for 20 minutes or until tender, then drain well. Add a little milk and mash until smooth.

3 Reduce the heat and continue cooking for a further 20 minutes, turning once or twice, or until the chicken is cooked right through. Test the thickest piece by cutting open and checking the meat is done.

4 Meanwhile, make the corn cakes. Stir the corn kernels into the cooled mashed potato and season with plenty of salt and pepper to taste. Using lightly floured hands, shape the mixture into 12 even-sized round cakes, each approximately 5cm/2in in diameter.

5 When the chicken breasts are cooked, use a draining spoon to remove them from the large frying pan and keep hot. Melt the butter in the pan and cook the corn cakes for about 3 minutes on each side, or until golden and heated through.

6 Meanwhile, mix together the sour cream with the chives in a small bowl to make a dip. Transfer the corn cakes from the frying pan to serving plates and top with the chicken breasts. Serve at once, offering the sour cream on the side.

NUTRITIONAL INFORMATION: Energy 505kcal/2119kJ; Protein 47.8g; Carbohydrate 32.2g, of which sugars 3.3g; Fat 21.5g, of which saturates 9.3g; Cholesterol 158mg; Calcium 61mg; Fibre 2.5g; Sodium 172mg.

Honey-glazed Chicken

This dish is popular in the USA and Australia and makes an easy meal served with baked potatoes.

ingredients

SERVES FOUR

- 4 boneless chicken breast portions (175g/6oz each)
- 15ml/1 tbsp sunflower oil
- 1 onion, chopped
- 1 garlic clove, crushed
- 45ml/3 tbsp clear honey
- 60ml/4 tbsp wholegrain mustard
- 60ml/4 tbsp orange juice
- 1 orange, peeled and segmented
- 30ml/2 tbsp soy sauce
- salt and ground black pepper
- fresh lemon balm or flat leaf parsley, to garnish
- mixed salad, to serve

1 Preheat the oven to 190°C/375°F/Gas 5. Season the chicken breast portions lightly with salt and pepper on both sides and place them, skin side up, in a single layer in a shallow roasting pan just large enough to accommodate them. Set the pan aside.

2 Heat the sunflower oil in a small pan over low heat. Add the chopped onion and garlic and cook, stirring occasionally, for about 2 minutes, until the vegetables are softened but not coloured.

3 Add the honey, mustard, orange juice, orange segments and soy sauce to the pan and cook, stirring constantly, until the honey has melted.

variations

- *Create a spicier version of this dish by substituting the same quantity of honey-flavoured mustard for the clear honey. Ensure the mustard has blended completely before pouring the sauce over the chicken.*

- *Substitute the juice of a lemon for the orange juice in the sauce.*

4 Pour the sauce over the chicken and bake, uncovered, for about 45 minutes, until the chicken is cooked through, basting once or twice with the cooking juices. Check by piercing the thickest part with the point of a knife; the juices should run clear.

5 Transfer the chicken to warmed individual plates, garnish with a few lemon balm leaves or flat leaf parsley and serve at once, accompanied by baked potatoes and a mixed salad.

NUTRITIONAL INFORMATION: Energy 251kcal/1062kJ; Protein 42.4g; Carbohydrate 10.5g, of which sugars 10.5g; Fat 4.7g, of which saturates 0.9g; Cholesterol 123mg; Calcium 12mg; Fibre 1g; Sodium 642mg.

Chicken Jambalaya

This New Orleans speciality is probably the best-known dish of Creole cuisine.

ingredients

SERVES FOUR

- 1.2kg/2½lb fresh chicken
- 1½ onions
- 1 bay leaf
- 4 black peppercorns
- 30ml/2 tbsp vegetable oil
- 2 garlic cloves, chopped
- 1 green (bell) pepper, chopped
- 1 celery stick, chopped
- 225g/8oz/1¼ cups long grain rice
- 115g/4oz chorizo sausage, sliced
- 115g/4oz/1 cup chopped cooked ham
- 400g/14oz can chopped tomatoes
- 2.5ml/½ tsp hot chilli powder
- 2.5ml/½ tsp cumin seeds
- 2.5ml/½ tsp ground cumin
- 5ml/1 tsp dried thyme
- 115g/4oz/1 cup cooked peeled prawns (shrimp)
- dash of Tabasco sauce
- salt and ground black pepper
- chopped fresh parsley, to garnish

1 Place the chicken in a large, heavy pan and pour in 600ml/ 1 pint/2½ cups water. Add half an onion, the bay leaf and the peppercorns and bring to the boil. Lower the heat, cover the pan and simmer for 1½ hours. Then lift the chicken out of the pan. Remove and discard the skin and bones and chop the meat. Strain the stock and reserve.

2 Chop the remaining whole onion. Heat the oil in a large frying pan over low heat. Add the onion, garlic, green pepper and celery and cook, stirring occasionally, for 5 minutes. Stir in the rice. Add the chorizo, ham and chicken and cook, stirring frequently, for 2–3 minutes.

3 Pour in the tomatoes and 300ml/½ pint/1¼ cups of the reserved stock and add the chilli, cumin and thyme. Bring to the boil, cover and simmer for 20 minutes, until the rice is tender and the liquid absorbed.

4 Stir in the prawns and Tabasco. Cook for 5 minutes more, then season to taste with salt and pepper and garnish with parsley.

cook's tip

Chicken thighs and drumsticks can be used for this dish.

NUTRITIONAL INFORMATION: Energy 802kcal/3340kJ; Protein 50.4g; Carbohydrate 59g, of which sugars 10.5g; Fat 40.5g, of which saturates 11.3g; Cholesterol 250mg; Calcium 104mg; Fibre 2.9g; Sodium 785mg.

Chicken Tagine

The combination of sweet and spicy flavours makes this Moroccan dish irresistible.

ingredients

SERVES FOUR

- 1.3kg/3lb chicken
- 3 garlic cloves, crushed
- small bunch of fresh coriander (cilantro), finely chopped
- juice of ½ lemon
- 5ml/1 tsp coarse salt
- 45ml/3 tbsp olive oil
- 1 large onion, grated
- pinch of saffron threads
- 5ml/1 tsp ground ginger
- 5ml/1 tsp ground black pepper
- 1 cinnamon stick
- 175g/6oz/1½ cups cracked green olives
- 2 preserved lemons, cut into strips
- steamed green vegetables, to serve
- 350g/12oz/2 cups couscous, to serve

1 Place the chicken in a deep dish. Rub the garlic, coriander, lemon juice and salt into the body cavity of the chicken. Mix the olive oil with the grated onion, saffron, ginger and pepper and rub this mixture over the outside of the chicken. Cover and leave to stand for about 30 minutes.

2 Transfer the chicken to a tagine or casserole dish and pour the marinating juices over. Pour in enough water to come halfway up the chicken, and bring to the boil.

3 Reduce the heat, cover and simmer for about 1 hour. Preheat the oven to 150°C/300°F/Gas 2. Using slotted spoons, lift the chicken out of the tagine or casserole dish and set aside on a plate, covered with foil. Keep warm.

4 Turn up the heat and boil the cooking liquid for 5 minutes to reduce it. Replace the chicken in the liquid and baste it thoroughly. Add the olives and preserved lemon and place the tagine or casserole in the oven for approximately 15 minutes.

5 Slice the chicken and serve immediately with plenty of steamed green vegetables and couscous.

cook's tip

A tagine is a traditional Morrocan earthenware pot with a conical lid which allows the food to cook in its own steam, ensuring that the meat remains tender.

NUTRITIONAL INFORMATION: Energy 585kcal/2422kJ; Protein 40.4g; Carbohydrate 0.4g, of which sugars 0.3g; Fat 46.7g, of which saturates 11.7g; Cholesterol 208mg; Calcium 68mg; Fibre 1.9g; Sodium 1151mg.

Chicken Curry

Curry powder comes in many varieties and degrees of heat. Use whichever type you prefer.

ingredients

SERVES FOUR

- 4 skinless chicken breast fillets
- 30ml/2 tbsp groundnut (peanut) oil
- 1 onion, thinly sliced
- 1 garlic clove, crushed
- 15ml/1 tbsp curry powder
- 25g/1oz/¼ cup plain (all-purpose) flour
- 450ml/¾ pint/scant 2 cups chicken stock
- 1 beefsteak tomato
- 15ml/1 tbsp mango chutney
- 15ml/1 tbsp lemon juice
- salt and ground black pepper
- basmatic rice, to serve

1 Cube the chicken breasts into evenly sized pieces. Heat the oil in a large heavy pan over medium heat. Add the chicken pieces and cook, turning frequently, for approximately 8–10 minutes, until evenly browned on both sides. Remove the chicken from the pan and keep warm.

2 Pour off some of the chicken fat if necessary and add the onion and garlic to the pan. Lower the heat and cook for approximately 5 minutes, until softened.

3 Stir in the curry powder and cook, stirring constantly, for a further 2 minutes. Stir in the flour and cook, stirring constantly, for 1 minute, then gradually blend in the chicken stock, stirring well between each addition to make a smooth sauce. Season to taste with salt and pepper.

4 Return the chicken pieces to the pan. Bring the curry sauce to the boil, then lower the heat, cover and simmer gently for 15 minutes, until the chicken is tender.

5 Skin the beefsteak tomato by blanching in boiling water for about 15 seconds, then running it under cold water to loosen the skin. Peel and dice.

6 Add to the chicken with the mango chutney and lemon juice. Heat through gently and adjust the seasoning to taste. Serve with basmati rice and Indian accompaniments.

cook's tip

Always fry curry powder before adding liquid to the dish.

NUTRITIONAL INFORMATION: Energy 571kcal/2392kJ; Protein 38.9g; Carbohydrate 78.9g, of which sugars 4g; Fat 10.8g, of which saturates 2g; Cholesterol 158mg; Calcium 43mg; Fibre 0.8g; Sodium 180mg.

Coq au Vin

Chicken is braised in red wine with bacon, mushrooms and onions in this classic dish.

ingredients

SERVES FOUR

- 50g/2oz/½ cup plain (all-purpose) flour
- 1.5kg/3–3½lb chicken, cut into 8 pieces
- 15ml/1 tbsp olive oil
- 65g/2½oz/5 tbsp butter
- 20 baby (pearl) onions
- 75g/3oz/½ cup diced streaky (fatty) bacon
- about 20 button (white) mushrooms
- 30ml/2 tbsp brandy
- 1 bottle red Burgundy wine
- bouquet garni
- 3 garlic cloves
- 5ml/1 tsp soft light brown sugar
- salt and ground black pepper
- 15ml/1 tbsp chopped fresh parsley, to garnish
- boiled new potatoes, to serve

1 Place 40g/1½oz/⅓ cup of the flour in a large plastic bag, season with salt and pepper and add the chicken pieces. Shake well to coat.

2 Heat the oil and 50g/2oz/4 tbsp of the butter in a large heavy pan over low heat. Add the onions and bacon and cook, stirring occasionally, for about 10 minutes, until the onions have browned lightly. Add the mushrooms and cook for 2 minutes. Remove the bacon and vegetables with a slotted spoon and reserve.

3 Add the chicken pieces, increase the heat and cook, turning frequently, for about 5–6 minutes, until evenly browned. Add the brandy and, standing well back, ignite it with a match. Shake the dish gently until the flames subside.

4 Add the wine, bouquet garni, garlic and sugar and season with salt and pepper. Bring to the boil, cover and simmer, stirring occasionally, for 1 hour. Add the onions, bacon and mushrooms, cover again and cook for 30 minutes.

5 Transfer the chicken, vegetables and bacon to a warmed dish. Remove the bouquet garni and boil the liquid for 2 minutes. Cream the remaining butter and flour. Whisk in spoonfuls of the mixture and cook to thicken. Pour the sauce over the chicken and serve garnished with parsley and new potatoes.

NUTRITIONAL INFORMATION: Energy 630kcal/2618kJ; Protein 42.8g; Carbohydrate 19.3g, of which sugars 7.4g; Fat 41g, of which saturates 17.3g; Cholesterol 209mg; Calcium 67mg; Fibre 2.6g; Sodium 480mg.

Turkey Bundles

These delicious turkey and cranberry filo pastry parcels are ideal for taking on a picnic.

ingredients

SERVES SIX

- 450g/1lb cooked turkey, cut into chunks
- 115g/4oz/1 cup Brie, diced
- 30ml/2 tbsp cranberry sauce
- 30ml/2 tbsp chopped fresh parsley
- 9 sheets filo pastry, 45 x 28cm/18 x 11in each, thawed if frozen
- 50g/2oz/¼ cup butter, melted
- salt and ground black pepper
- green salad, to serve

variations

These little parcels can be made with a variety of fillings and are great for using up left-over cooked meats.

• To make Ham and Cheddar Bundles, replace the turkey with ham and use Cheddar in place of the Brie. A fruit-flavoured chutney is a good alternative to the cranberry sauce.

• To make Chicken and Stilton Bundles, use cooked chicken in place of the turkey and white Stilton instead of Brie. Replace the cranberry sauce with mango chutney.

• To make Chicken and Corn Bundles, use cooked chicken with cooked corn. Replace the cranberry chutney with mayonnaise.

1 Preheat the oven to 200°C/400°F/Gas 6. Mix together the cooked turkey, diced Brie, cranberry sauce and chopped fresh parsley. Season well with salt and ground black pepper.

2 Cut the filo sheets in half widthways and trim to make 18 squares. Layer three pieces of pastry together, gently brushing them with a little melted butter so that they stick together. Repeat with the remaining filo squares to give six pieces.

3 Divide the turkey mixture among the pastry, making neat piles on each piece. Gather up the pastry to enclose the filling in neat bundles. Place on a baking sheet, brush with a little melted butter and bake for 20 minutes, or until the pastry is crisp and golden. Serve hot or warm with a green salad.

cook's tip

Filo pastry dries out quickly, so keep squares not currently being used covered under a clean damp dish towel, and work quickly.

NUTRITIONAL INFORMATION: Energy 304kcal/1274kJ; Protein 27.3g; Carbohydrate 16.6g, of which sugars 3.9g; Fat 14.3g, of which saturates 8.5g; Cholesterol 95mg; Calcium 91mg; Fibre 0.3g; Sodium 204mg.

Chicken & Leek Pie

A filling pie with a two-cheese sauce, this dish is ideal for serving on a cold winter's day.

ingredients

SERVES FOUR TO SIX

- 3 skinless chicken breast fillets
- 1 carrot, thickly sliced
- 1 small onion, quartered
- 6 black peppercorns
- 1 bouquet garni
- 450g/1lb shortcrust pastry dough, thawed if frozen
- 50g/2oz/¼ cup butter
- 2 leeks, thinly sliced
- 50g/2oz/¼ cup grated Cheddar cheese
- 25g/1oz/⅓ cup freshly grated Parmesan cheese
- 45ml/3 tbsp chopped fresh parsley
- 30ml/2 tbsp wholegrain mustard
- 5ml/1 tsp cornflour (cornstarch)
- 300ml/½ pint/1¼ cups double (heavy) cream
- beaten egg, to glaze
- salt and ground black pepper
- mixed green salad leaves, to serve

1 Put the chicken, carrot, onion, peppercorns and bouquet garni in a pan, cover with water and poach gently, for 20–30 minutes, until tender. Leave the chicken to cool in the liquid, then drain and cut into strips.

2 Preheat the oven to 200°C/400°F/Gas 6. Divide the dough into two pieces, one slightly larger than the other. Use the larger piece to line an 18 x 28cm/7 x 11in baking tin (pan). Prick the base and bake for 15 minutes, then leave to cool.

3 Melt the butter in a frying pan over low heat. Add the leeks and cook, stirring occasionally, for 5–8 minutes, until soft. Stir in the cheeses and the parsley.

4 Spread half the leek mixture over the pastry base, cover with the chicken strips in an even layer, then top with the remaining leek mixture.

5 Mix together the mustard, cornflour and cream in a bowl. Season with salt and pepper and pour into the pie.

6 Moisten the pastry base edges. Use the remaining pastry to cover the pie. Brush with beaten egg and bake for 30–40 minutes, until golden and crisp. Serve with salad.

NUTRITIONAL INFORMATION: Energy 620kcal/2584kJ; Protein 28.2g; Carbohydrate 39.4g, of which sugars 3.2g; Fat 39.7g, of which saturates 24.1g; Cholesterol 151mg; Calcium 237mg; Fibre 3.3g; Sodium 218mg.

Tandoori Chicken Kebabs

This dish originates from the Punjab, where it is traditionally cooked in clay ovens known as tandoors.

ingredients

SERVES FOUR

- 4 skinless chicken breast fillets (about 175g/6oz each)
- 15ml/1 tbsp lemon juice
- 45ml/3 tbsp tandoori paste
- 45ml/3 tbsp plain yogurt
- 1 garlic clove, crushed
- 30ml/2 tbsp chopped fresh coriander (cilantro)
- 1 onion, cut into wedges and separated into layers
- vegetable oil, for brushing
- salt and ground black pepper
- fresh coriander sprigs, to garnish
- pilau rice and naan bread, to serve

1 Chop the chicken breast fillets into 2.5cm/1in dice and place the pieces in a bowl. Add the lemon juice, tandoori paste, yogurt, garlic and coriander and season with salt and pepper. Stir well. Cover the bowl with clear film (plastic wrap) and leave the chicken to marinate in the refrigerator, stirring occasionally, for 2–3 hours.

variation

Use fresh coriander (cilantro) as an alternative to the chopped fresh mint in the yogurt dip.

2 Preheat the grill (broiler). Thread alternate pieces of marinated chicken and onion on to four large skewers. Brush the pieces of onion with a little oil. Lay the kebabs on a grill rack and cook under high heat for 10–12 minutes, turning once.

3 Transfer to warmed plates, garnish the kebabs with fresh coriander and serve at once with pilau rice and naan bread.

cook's tip

For a special occasion, or when barbecuing, serve with a yogurt dip. Mix together 250ml/8fl oz/1 cup natural (plain) yogurt, 30ml/2 tbsp double (heavy) cream, 30ml/2 tbsp chopped fresh mint and 1/2 peeled, seeded and finely chopped cucumber in a bowl. Season to taste. Cover with clear film (plastic wrap) and chill until ready to serve.

NUTRITIONAL INFORMATION: Energy 222kcal/937kJ; Protein 42.8g; Carbohydrate 2g, of which sugars 1.7g; Fat 4.8g, of which saturates 0.9g; Cholesterol 123mg; Calcium 34mg; Fibre 0.2g; Sodium 115mg.

Golden Parmesan Chicken

Served cold with the garlic mayonnaise, these morsels of chicken make fabulous picnic food.

ingredients

SERVES FOUR

- 4 skinless, boneless chicken breast portions
- 75g/3oz/1½ cups fresh white breadcrumbs
- 40g/1½oz/½ cup finely grated Parmesan cheese
- 30ml/2 tbsp chopped fresh parsley
- 2 eggs, lightly beaten
- 50g/2oz/4 tbsp butter, melted
- salt and ground black pepper
- green salad, to serve

For the garlic mayonnaise

- 120ml/4fl oz/½ cup good-quality mayonnaise
- 120ml/4fl oz/½ cup fromage frais (farmer's cheese)
- 1–2 garlic cloves, crushed

1 Using a sharp knife, cut each chicken breast portion into four or five large, even-sized pieces. Mix together the breadcrumbs, grated Parmesan cheese and chopped parsley in a shallow dish and season well with salt and pepper.

2 Dip the chicken pieces in the beaten egg, then into the breadcrumb mixture. Place the pieces in a single layer on a baking sheet and put in the refrigerator to chill for at least 30 minutes.

3 Meanwhile, make the garlic mayonnaise. Mix together the mayonnaise, fromage frais and garlic and season with pepper to taste. Spoon the mayonnaise into a small serving bowl, cover with clear film (plastic wrap) and chill in the refrigerator until ready to serve.

4 Preheat the oven to 180°C/350°F/Gas 4. Drizzle the melted butter over the chicken pieces and cook in the oven for about 20 minutes, until crisp and golden. Serve the chicken immediately with a crisp green salad and the garlic mayonnaise for dipping. Alternatively, transfer the chicken to a rack and leave to cool. Store in the refrigerator until required, then serve at room temperature with a green salad and the garlic mayonnaise.

NUTRITIONAL INFORMATION: Energy 625kcal/2608kJ; Protein 48g; Carbohydrate 17.2g, of which sugars 3g; Fat 41.1g, of which saturates 13.3g; Cholesterol 260mg; Calcium 199mg; Fibre 0.5g; Sodium 598mg.

Duck & Avocado Salad

Duck breasts glazed with honey and soy sauce are served warm with fresh raspberries and avocado.

ingredients

SERVES FOUR

- 4 small or 2 large duck breast portions, halved if large
- 15ml/1 tbsp clear honey
- 15ml/1 tbsp dark soy sauce
- mixed chopped fresh salad leaves such as lamb's lettuce, radicchio or frisée
- 2 medium avocados, stoned (pitted), peeled and cut into chunks
- 115g/4oz/1 cup raspberries
- salt and ground black pepper

For the dressing

- 60ml/4 tbsp olive oil
- 15ml/1 tbsp raspberry vinegar
- 15ml/1 tbsp redcurrant jelly

1 Preheat the oven to 220°C/425°F/Gas 7. Prick the skin of each duck breast portion with a fork. Blend the honey and soy sauce together in a small bowl, then brush the mixture all over the skin of the duck portions.

2 Place the duck breast portions on a rack set over a roasting pan and season with salt and pepper. Roast at the top of the hot oven for 15–20 minutes, until the skins are crisp and the meat is cooked through. (Save the duck fat for another dish, such as roast potatoes or vegetables.)

3 Meanwhile, to make the salad dressing, put the oil, vinegar and redcurrant jelly in a small bowl, season with salt and pepper and whisk well until evenly blended.

4 Arrange the salad leaves on four individual plates and distribute the avocados and raspberries between them. Slice the duck breast portions diagonally and arrange on the salad leaves. Spoon the dressing over the top and serve the salad immediately.

cook's tip

Hass or Ryan avocados have the most flavour and a good texture. Store avocados in a paper bag at room temperature to ripen: do not put them in the refrigerator.

NUTRITIONAL INFORMATION: Energy 345kcal/1438kJ; Protein 21.2g; Carbohydrate 8g, of which sugars 7.3g; Fat 27.2g, of which saturates 5g; Cholesterol 110mg; Calcium 26mg; Fibre 2.4g; Sodium 382mg.

Normandy Pheasant

Calvados, cider, apples and cream – the produce of Normandy – make this a flavoursome dish.

ingredients

SERVES FOUR

- 2 oven-ready pheasants
- 15ml/1 tbsp olive oil
- 25g/1oz/2 tbsp unsalted butter
- 60ml/4 tbsp Calvados or applejack
- 450ml/¾ pint/scant 2 cups dry (hard) cider
- 1 bouquet garni
- 3 eating apples
- 150ml/¼ pint/⅔ cup double (heavy) cream
- salt and ground black pepper
- a few sprigs of fresh thyme, to garnish

1 Cut each pheasant into four pieces. Discard the backbones and knuckle bones and any excess skin.

2 Heat the oil and butter in a large heavy pan and brown the pheasant in batches over a high heat. Return the pieces to the pan when they are all browned.

cook's tip

Tiny balls of lead shot can be left in game birds. Rub your fingertips over the surface to locate any small hard balls and cut out.

3 Standing well back, pour over the Calvados or applejack and ignite it with a match. Shake the pan and when the flames have subsided, pour in the cider, then add the bouquet garni and season to taste with salt and pepper. Bring to the boil, cover with a tight-fitting lid and simmer for about 50 minutes.

4 Core and thickly slice the apples. Tuck the apple slices around the pheasant. Cover and cook for 5–10 minutes, or until the pheasant is tender.

5 Lift out the pheasant pieces and apples with a slotted spoon and transfer to a warmed serving plate. Keep warm.

6 Remove and discard the bouquet garni, then boil the sauce rapidly to reduce by half to a syrupy consistency. Stir in the cream and simmer for a further 2–3 minutes, until thickened. Taste the sauce and adjust the seasoning, if necessary. Spoon the sauce over the pheasant pieces and serve immediately, garnished with fresh thyme sprigs.

NUTRITIONAL INFORMATION: Energy 805kcal/3347kJ; Protein 58.8g; Carbohydrate 8.1g, of which sugars 8.1g; Fat 52.9g, of which saturates 24.6g; Cholesterol 525mg; Calcium 91mg; Fibre 0.8g; Sodium 191mg.

Beef Casserole

Use a full-bodied red wine such as a Burgundy to create the flavoursome sauce in this casserole.

ingredients

SERVES FOUR TO SIX

- 900g/2lb braising steak, cut into cubes
- 2 onions, coarsely chopped
- 1 bouquet garni
- 6 black peppercorns
- 15ml/1 tbsp red wine vinegar
- 1 bottle red wine
- 45ml/3 tbsp olive oil
- 3 celery sticks, thickly sliced
- 50g/2oz/½ cup plain (all-purpose) flour
- 300ml/½ pint/1¼ cups beef stock
- 30ml/2 tbsp tomato purée (paste)
- 2 garlic cloves, crushed
- 175g/6oz wild or cultivated mushrooms, sliced
- 400g/14oz can artichoke hearts, drained and halved
- chopped fresh parsley and thyme, to garnish

1 Put the meat, onions, bouquet garni, peppercorns, vinegar and wine in a bowl. Cover with clear film (plastic wrap) and leave to marinate in the refrigerator overnight.

2 The next day, preheat the oven to 160°C/325°F/Gas 3. Drain the meat, reserving the marinade, and pat dry. Heat the oil in a large flameproof casserole. Add the meat and onions, in batches, and cook, stirring, until the meat is evenly browned. Remove and set aside.

3 Add the celery to the casserole and cook, stirring frequently, until browned, then remove and set aside with the meat and onions.

4 Sprinkle the flour into the oil remaining in the casserole and cook, stirring constantly, for 1 minute. Gradually add the reserved marinade and the stock, stirring constantly, and bring the mixture to the boil. Return the meat, onions and celery to the casserole, then stir in the tomato purée and the crushed garlic.

5 Cover the casserole with a tight-fitting lid and cook in the oven for about 2¼ hours. Stir in the mushrooms and artichokes, cover again and cook for a further 15 minutes, until the meat is tender. Garnish with parsley and thyme, and serve hot with mashed potatoes, if you like.

NUTRITIONAL INFORMATION: Energy 367kcal/1529kJ; Protein 35.3g; Carbohydrate 6.9g, of which sugars 5.7g; Fat 19.6g, of which saturates 6.4g; Cholesterol 87mg; Calcium 32mg; Fibre 1.2g; Sodium 119mg.

Boeuf Bourguignon

This classic French dish comes from Burgundy, where the local red wine is used to flavour it.

ingredients

SERVES FOUR

- 30ml/2 tbsp olive oil
- 225g/8oz piece streaky (fatty) bacon, diced
- 12 baby (pearl) onions
- 900g/2lb braising steak
- 1 large onion, thickly sliced
- 15g/½oz/2 tbsp plain (all-purpose) flour
- about 450ml/¾ pint/scant 2 cups red Burgundy wine
- 1 bouquet garni
- 1 garlic clove
- 225g/8oz button (white) mushrooms, halved
- salt and ground black pepper
- chopped parsley, to garnish

1 Heat the oil in a large, heavy pan over low heat. Add the bacon and baby onions and cook, stirring occasionally, for 7–8 minutes, until the onions are evenly browned and the bacon fat has become translucent. Remove with a slotted spoon and set aside on a plate.

cook's tip

Try to buy braising steak that is marbled with fat, as this will melt into the sauce during cooking to give the dish a delicious flavour.

2 Cut the braising steak into large cubes. Add the beef to the pan, increase the heat to medium and cook, stirring frequently, until evenly browned all over. Add the sliced onion and cook, stirring occasionally, for 4–5 minutes.

3 Sprinkle in the flour and cook, stirring constantly, for 1 minute. Gradually stir in the wine, add the bouquet garni and garlic and season with salt and pepper. Bring to the boil, cover with a tight-fitting lid and simmer for 2 hours.

4 Stir in the reserved baby onions and bacon and add a little extra wine if the liquid in the casserole has reduced too much. Add the mushrooms. Replace the lid of the pan and cook for a further 30 minutes, or until the meat is very tender.

5 Remove from the heat. Remove and discard the bouquet garni and the garlic. Taste and adjust the seasoning, if necessary, then ladle the stew on to warmed plates, garnish with chopped fresh parsley and serve immediately.

NUTRITIONAL INFORMATION: Energy 749kcal/3117kJ; Protein 63.3g; Carbohydrate 15.2g, of which sugars 8.8g; Fat 40.3g, of which saturates 14g; Cholesterol 167mg; Calcium 69mg; Fibre 2.8g; Sodium 868mg.

Steak & Kidney Pie

This recipe for a traditional British dish includes mushrooms to add extra richness to the gravy.

ingredients

SERVES FOUR

- 30ml/2 tbsp sunflower oil
- 1 onion, chopped
- 115g/4oz bacon, finely chopped
- 500g/1¼lb braising steak
- 25g/1oz/¼ cup plain (all-purpose) flour
- 115g/4oz lamb's kidneys
- large bouquet garni
- 400ml/14fl oz/1¾ cups beef stock
- 115g/4oz button (white) mushrooms
- 225g/8oz puff pastry dough
- beaten egg, to glaze
- salt and ground black pepper

1 Preheat the oven to 160°C/325°F/Gas 3. Heat the oil in a heavy pan over low heat. Add the onion and bacon and cook, stirring occasionally, for about 8 minutes, until lightly browned.

2 Dice the steak and toss in the flour. Stir the meat into the pan, in batches, and cook, stirring frequently, until evenly browned. Toss the kidneys in flour, add to the pan with the bouquet garni and cook briefly, stirring occasionally, until they are browned.

3 Transfer the meat and onions to a casserole, pour in the stock, cover with a tight-fitting lid and cook in the oven for 2 hours. Remove the casserole from the oven, stir in the mushrooms, season with salt and pepper and leave to cool.

4 Preheat the oven to 220°C/425°F/Gas 7. Roll out the pastry to 2cm/¾in larger than the top of a 1.2 litre/2 pint/5 cup pie dish. Cut off a pastry strip and fit it around the dampened rim of the dish. Brush the strip with water.

5 Turn the meat mixture into the dish. Lay the pastry over the dish, press the edges together to seal, then knock them up with the back of a knife. Make a small slit in the pastry lid, brush with beaten egg and bake for 20 minutes, then lower the oven temperature to 180°C/350°F/Gas 4 and bake for a further 20 minutes, until the pastry is golden and crisp.

variation

Omit the kidneys and replace with extra braising steak.

NUTRITIONAL INFORMATION: Energy 597kcal/2488kJ; Protein 42.5g; Carbohydrate 27g, of which sugars 1.7g; Fat 36.7g, of which saturates 7.5g; Cholesterol 178mg; Calcium 57mg; Fibre 0.7g; Sodium 742mg.

Sizzling Beef & Celeriac

The crisp celeriac batons look like fine pieces of straw when cooked and have a celery-like flavour.

ingredients

SERVES FOUR

- 450g/1lb celeriac
- 150ml/¼ pint/⅔ cup vegetable oil
- 1 red (bell) pepper
- 6 spring onions (scallions)
- 450g/1lb rump (round) or sirloin steak
- 60ml/4 tbsp beef stock
- 30ml/2 tbsp rice or sherry vinegar
- 10ml/2 tsp Worcestershire sauce
- 10ml/2 tsp tomato purée (paste)
- salt and ground black pepper

1 Peel the celeriac and then cut it into fine batons, using a cleaver if you have one or a large sharp knife.

2 Heat a wok, then add two-thirds of the oil. When the oil is hot, add the celeriac batons, in batches, and stir-fry until golden brown and crisp. Drain well on kitchen paper. Discard the oil.

3 Cut the red pepper and the spring onions into 2.5cm/1in lengths, cutting diagonally. Cut the steak into strips, across the grain of the meat.

4 Wipe out the wok with kitchen paper and return it to the heat. Add the remaining oil. When the oil is hot, add the prepared red pepper and spring onions and stir-fry for 2–3 minutes until beginning to brown but still crisp.

5 Add the steak strips and stir-fry for a further 3–4 minutes, until well browned. Add the stock, vinegar, Worcestershire sauce and tomato purée. Season well with salt and pepper and serve with the celeriac "straw".

cook's tip

The Chinese use a large cleaver for preparing most vegetables. This looks fearsome, but with a little practice, you will discover that it is the ideal kitchen utensil for cutting fine vegetable batons and chopping meat into thin, even strips.

NUTRITIONAL INFORMATION: Energy 318kcal/1324kJ; Protein 26.2g; Carbohydrate 5g, of which sugars 4.8g; Fat 21.6g, of which saturates 3.9g; Cholesterol 66mg; Calcium 66mg; Fibre 2.2g; Sodium 174mg.

Irish Stew

This wholesome and filling stew is given a slight piquancy by the inclusion of a little anchovy sauce.

1 Preheat the oven to 160°C/325°F/Gas 3. Dice the bacon and then cook in a heavy frying pan, without any added fat, over medium-low heat for 3–5 minutes, until the fat runs. Add the celery and one-third of the onions and cook, stirring occasionally, for about 10 minutes, until the vegetables are softened and browned.

2 Layer the lamb chops, potatoes, vegetable and bacon mixture and remaining onions in a heavy casserole, seasoning each layer with salt and pepper as you go. Finish with a layer of potatoes.

3 Pour the veal stock, Worcestershire sauce and anchovy sauce into the cooking juices in the pan. Bring to the boil, stirring constantly. Pour the mixture into the casserole, adding water, if necessary, so that the liquid comes halfway up the sides of the casserole.

4 Cover the casserole with a tight-fitting lid, then cook in the oven for 3 hours or more, until the meat and vegetables are very tender. Taste and correct the seasoning if necessary.

5 Serve the dish immediately, sprinkled with chopped fresh parsley. Alternatively, leave it to cool, then chill in the refrigerator overnight. Next day, spoon off any fat that has solidified on the surface of the stew, then reheat thoroughly in the oven or on the stove before serving.

cook's tip

If you don't have any anchovy sauce, chop 2–3 anchovy fillets and add them to the dish.

NUTRITIONAL INFORMATION: Energy 823kcal/3453kJ; Protein 80g; Carbohydrate 50.3g, of which sugars 10.4g; Fat 34.9g, of which saturates 14.8g; Cholesterol 266mg; Calcium 137mg; Fibre 4.4g; Sodium 540mg.

Butterflied Leg of Lamb

A seasoning of ground cumin and garlic gives the lamb a wonderful Middle Eastern flavour.

ingredients

SERVES SIX

- 1.75kg/4lb leg of lamb
- 60ml/4 tbsp extra virgin olive oil
- 30ml/2 tbsp ground cumin
- 4–6 garlic cloves, crushed
- salt and ground black pepper
- fresh coriander (cilantro) sprigs and lemon wedges, to garnish
- mixed salad leaves and pitta bread, to serve

1 To butterfly the lamb, cut away the meat from the bone using a small sharp knife. Remove any excess fat and the thin, parchment-like membrane. Flatten the meat with a rolling pin to an even thickness, then prick the fleshy side of the lamb well with the tip of a knife. Place the lamb in a large, shallow dish.

2 Mix together the olive oil, cumin and garlic in a bowl and season with pepper. Spoon the mixture all over the lamb, then rub it well into the crevices. Cover the dish with clear film (plastic wrap) and place the lamb in the refrigerator to marinate overnight.

3 Preheat the oven to 200°C/400°F/Gas 6. Spread the lamb, skin side up, on a rack in a roasting pan. Season with salt and roast for 45–60 minutes, until brown on the outside but still pink in the centre.

4 Remove the lamb from the roasting pan and place on a board. Cover with foil and leave it in a warm place to rest for about 10 minutes. Cut the lamb into diagonal slices, place on warmed plates and garnish with fresh coriander sprigs and lemon wedges. Serve at once with a mixed salad and pitta breads.

variation

For a Provençal flavour, omit the ground cumin and add fresh rosemary to the marinade.

cook's tips

• Butterflying is a technique used to create a flatter, thinner piece of meat that will cook evenly in a shorter time.

• The butterflied lamb may be cooked on the barbecue rather than roasted in the oven. Thread it on to two long skewers and grill it over hot coals for 20–25 minutes on each side.

NUTRITIONAL INFORMATION: Energy 505kcal/2106kJ; Protein 59.8g; Carbohydrate 0g, of which sugars 0g; Fat 29.5g, of which saturates 12.8g; Cholesterol 225mg; Calcium 23mg; Fibre 0g; Sodium 128mg.

Lamb with Mint Sauce

This tasty and quickly prepared dish uses the classic British combination of lamb and mint.

ingredients

SERVES FOUR

- 8 lamb noisettes, 2–2.5cm/ ¾–1in thick
- 30ml/2 tbsp vegetable oil
- 45ml/3 tbsp medium-bodied dry white wine, or vegetable or veal stock
- salt and ground black pepper
- fresh mint sprigs, to garnish
- fresh vegetables, to serve

For the sauce

- 30ml/2 tbsp boiling water
- 5ml/1 tsp sugar, to taste
- leaves from a small bunch of fresh mint, finely chopped
- about 30ml/2 tbsp white wine vinegar

1 To make the mint sauce, stir the boiling water and sugar together in a heatproof bowl until the sugar is dissolved, then add the mint leaves and vinegar to taste. Season with salt and pepper. Leave to stand for 30 minutes.

cook's tip

In the past, cooks used more sugar to counteract the sharpness of the vinegar in the mint sauce: add more sugar if you like. It was also common to sprinkle the mint leaves with 5ml/1 tsp sugar before chopping them.

2 Season the lamb with pepper. Heat the oil in a large, heavy frying pan. Add the lamb, in batches if necessary so that the pan is not crowded, and cook for about 3 minutes on each side for meat that is pink in the middle.

3 Transfer the lamb noisettes, as they are done to your liking, to a warmed plate and season, then cover and keep warm while you make the gravy.

4 Stir the wine or stock into the cooking juices, scraping up the sediment from the base of the pan, and bring to the boil. Leave to bubble for a couple of minutes, then pour over the lamb. Garnish the lamb noisettes with small sprigs of mint and serve hot with the mint sauce and fresh vegetables.

NUTRITIONAL INFORMATION: Energy 332kcal/1384kJ; Protein 29.6g; Carbohydrate 1.6g, of which sugars 1.4g; Fat 22.3g, of which saturates 8.5g; Cholesterol 114mg; Calcium 22mg; Fibre 0g; Sodium 130mg.

Lamb with Apricots

Inspired by Middle Eastern cooking, this fruity, spicy casserole is simple to make yet looks impressive.

ingredients

SERVES FOUR

- 115g/4oz dried apricots
- 50g/2oz/scant ½ cup seedless raisins
- 2.5ml/½ tsp saffron threads
- 150ml/¼ pint/⅔ cup orange juice
- 15ml/1 tbsp red wine vinegar
- 30–45ml/2–3 tbsp olive oil
- 1.5kg/3–3½ lb leg of lamb, boned
- 1 onion, chopped
- 2 garlic cloves, crushed
- 10ml/2 tsp ground cumin
- 1.25ml/¼ tsp ground cloves
- 15ml/1 tbsp ground coriander
- 25g/1oz/¼ cup plain (all-purpose) flour
- 600ml/1 pint/2½ cups lamb or chicken stock
- 45ml/3 tbsp chopped fresh coriander (cilantro)
- salt and ground black pepper
- saffron rice mixed with toasted almonds and fresh coriander, to serve

1 Mix together the dried apricots, raisins, saffron, orange juice and vinegar in a bowl. Cover with clear film (plastic wrap) and leave to soak for 2–3 hours. Cut the lamb into 2.5cm/1in cubes.

2 Heat 30ml/2 tbsp oil in a large heavy pan over medium heat. Add the cubed lamb, in small batches, and cook, stirring frequently, for 5–8 minutes, until evenly browned on all sides. Remove the cooked lamb with a slotted spoon and set aside.

3 Add a little more oil to the pan, if necessary, and lower the heat. Add the onion and garlic and cook, stirring occasionally, for 5 minutes, until the vegetables are softened but not coloured.

4 Stir in the spices and flour and cook, stirring, for 1–2 minutes more. Return the meat to the pan. Stir in the stock, fresh coriander and the soaked fruit with its liquid. Season to taste with salt and pepper, then bring to the boil. Cover the pan with a tight-fitting lid, lower the heat and simmer for about 1½ hours (adding extra stock if necessary), or until the lamb is tender. Serve with saffron rice mixed with toasted almonds and fresh coriander.

NUTRITIONAL INFORMATION: Energy 765kcal/3192kJ; Protein 58.5g; Carbohydrate 27.5g, of which sugars 23.4g; Fat 47.5g, of which saturates 14.7g; Cholesterol 218mg; Calcium 53mg; Fibre 2.5g; Sodium 181mg.

Lamb Kebabs

Delicious skewered lamb stuffed into a pitta is a popular fast food in Greece and Turkey.

ingredients

SERVES FOUR

- 300ml/½ pint/1¼ cups Greek (US strained plain) yogurt
- ½ garlic clove, crushed
- generous pinch of saffron powder
- 30ml/2 tbsp chopped fresh mint
- 30ml/2 tbsp clear honey
- 45ml/3 tbsp olive oil
- 3 lamb neck (US shoulder) fillets (about 675g/1½lb total)
- 2 red or yellow (bell) pappers, cut into 2.5cm/1in cubes
- whole baby onions
- salt and ground black pepper
- small fresh mint leaves, to garnish
- mixed salad and Lebanese flat bread or pitta bread, to serve

1 Mix together the yogurt, garlic, saffron, mint, honey and most of the oil in a shallow dish and season with pepper.

2 Trim the lamb and cut into 2.5cm/1in cubes. Stir into the marinade. Cover with clear film (plastic wrap) and leave to marinate in the refrigerator for at least 4 hours or overnight.

3 Preheat the grill (broiler). Drain the lamb and reserve the marinade. Thread the lamb, peppers and baby onions alternately on to metal or wooden skewers. (If you are using wooden skewers, soak them in water for 30 minutes first to prevent them from charring during cooking.) Use four or eight skewers, depending on their size.

4 Lightly brush the kebabs with a little of the reserved olive oil to keep the meat succulent and tender when being cooked.

5 Grill (broil) the kebabs for approximately 10–12 minutes, turning and basting occasionally with the reserved marinade, until the lamb and vegetables are tender. Alternatively, cook the kebabs on the barbecue.

6 Transfer the skewers to warmed plates and serve, accompanied by a mixed salad and hot Lebanese flat bread or pitta bread.

cook's tip

To make a more substantial meal, serve the kebabs on a bed of flavoured rice or couscous.

NUTRITIONAL INFORMATION: Energy 526kcal/2194kJ; Protein 39.7g; Carbohydrate 15.4g, of which sugars 13.4g; Fat 35.4g, of which saturates 14g; Cholesterol 128mg; Calcium 155mg; Fibre 3.1g; Sodium 204mg.

Pot-roasted Lamb

This slow-braised dish of lamb and tomatoes is perfect for a family lunch or supper with friends.

ingredients

SERVES EIGHT

- 1kg/2¼lb lamb on the bone
- 8 garlic cloves, chopped
- 2.5–5ml/½–1 tsp ground cumin
- 45ml/3 tbsp olive oil
- juice of 1 lemon
- 2 onions, thinly sliced
- about 500ml/17fl oz/2¼ cups lamb, beef or vegetable stock
- 75–90ml/5–6 tbsp tomato purée (paste)
- 1 cinnamon stick
- 2–3 large pinches of ground allspice or ground cloves
- 15–30ml/1–2 tbsp sugar
- 400g/14oz/scant 3 cups runner (green) beans
- salt and ground black pepper
- 15m–30ml/1–2 tbsp chopped fresh parsley, to garnish

1 Preheat the oven to 160°C/325°F/Gas 3. Coat the lamb with the garlic, cumin, olive oil, lemon juice, salt and ground black pepper, rubbing it into the flesh well.

variations

• Adding (bell) peppers would give this dish added sweetness. Use green peppers for a more savoury flavour.

• For a more Mediterranean taste, add sliced green olives stuffed with pimiento or a small spoonful of chopped capers to the sauce.

2 Heat a flameproof casserole that is a sufficient size to take all the ingredients. Sear the lamb on all sides. Add the onions and pour the stock over the meat to cover. Stir in the tomator purée, spices and sugar. Cover and cook in the oven for 2–3 hours.

3 Remove the casserole from the oven and pour the stock into a pan. Move the onions to the side of the dish and return to the oven, uncovered for a further 20 minutes to burn off the excess fluid.

4 Meanwhile, add the beans to the hot stock and cook until the beans are tender and the sauce has thickened. Slice the meat and serve with the pan juices and beans. Garnish with parsley.

cook's tip

Cooking the lamb while still on the bone ensures that none of the flavour is lost.

NUTRITIONAL INFORMATION: Energy 371kcal/1554kJ; Protein 26.3g; Carbohydrate 7.9g, of which sugars 6.5g; Fat 26.4g, of which saturates 10.9g; Cholesterol 104mg; Calcium 40mg; Fibre 1.9g; Sodium 103mg.

Roast Stuffed Pork

Serve this perfect Sunday lunch dish with fresh vegetables, roast potatoes and apple sauce.

ingredients

SERVES SIX TO EIGHT

- 1.3–1.6kg/3–3½lb boneless loin of pork
- 60ml/4 tbsp dry breadcrumbs
- 10ml/2 tsp chopped fresh sage
- 25ml/1½ tbsp plain (all-purpose) flour
- 300ml/½ pint/1¼ cups (hard) cider
- 150ml/¼ pint/⅔ cup water
- 10ml/2 tsp redcurrant jelly
- salt and ground black pepper

For the stuffing

- 25g/1oz/2 tbsp butter
- 50g/2oz bacon, chopped
- 2 large onions, finely chopped
- 75g/3oz/1½ cups fresh white breadcrumbs
- 30ml/2 tbsp chopped fresh sage
- 5ml/1 tsp chopped fresh thyme
- 10ml/2 tsp grated lemon rind
- 1 small egg, beaten

1 Preheat the oven to 220°C/425°F/Gas 7. To make the stuffing, melt the butter and fry the bacon until it begins to brown. Add the onions and cook gently until softened but not browned. Mix with the breadcrumbs, sage, thyme, lemon rind and egg, then season with salt and pepper.

2 Cut the rind off the joint of pork in one piece and score it well. Place the pork fat-side down and season. Add a layer of stuffing, then roll up and tie neatly.

3 Lay the rind over the pork and rub in 5ml/1 tsp salt. Roast for 2–2½ hours, reducing the temperature to 190°C/375°F/Gas 5 after 20 minutes. Shape the remaining stuffing into balls and add to the roasting pan for the last 30 minutes. Remove the rind from the pork. Increase the temperature to 220°C/425°F/Gas 7 and roast the rind for a further 20–25 minutes, until crisp. Mix the breadcrumbs and sage and press them into the pork fat. Cook the pork for 10 minutes, then leave in a warm place for 15–20 minutes.

4 Remove all but 30–45ml/2–3 tbsp of the fat from the pan. Place over medium heat and stir in the flour, cider and water. Cook for 10 minutes. Strain into a clean pan, add the jelly and cook for 5 minutes. Serve with the pork and crackling.

NUTRITIONAL INFORMATION: Energy 446Kcal/1874kJ; Protein 52.8g; Carbohydrate 26.4g, of which sugars 5.1g; Fat 15.1g, of which saturates 6g; Cholesterol 185mg; Calcium 76mg; Fibre 1.7g; Sodium 479mg.

Somerset Pork & Apple

A creamy cider sauce accompanies tender pieces of pork and sliced apples in a rich supper dish.

ingredients

SERVES FOUR

- 25g/1oz/2 tbsp butter
- 500g/1¼lb pork loin, cut into bitesize pieces
- 12 baby (pearl) onions, peeled
- 10ml/2 tsp grated lemon rind
- 300ml/½ pint/1¼ cups dry (hard) cider
- 150ml/¼ pint/⅔ cup veal stock
- 2 crisp eating apples such as Granny Smith, sliced
- 45ml/3 tbsp chopped fresh parsley
- 100ml/3½fl oz/scant ½ cup whipping cream
- salt and ground black pepper

1 Melt the butter in a large sauté or frying pan over medium heat. Add the pork, in batches, and cook, stirring frequently, for about 8 minutes, until browned all over. Transfer the pork to a bowl with a slotted spoon.

2 Add the onions to the pan and lower the heat. Cook, stirring occasionally, for 8–10 minutes, until lightly browned.

3 Stir in the lemon rind, cider and stock, bring to the boil and cook for about 3 minutes. Return all the pork to the pan, cover and simmer gently for about 25 minutes, until tender. Add the apples to the pan and cook for a further 5 minutes. Using a slotted spoon, transfer the pork, onions and apples to a warmed serving dish, cover and keep warm.

4 Stir the parsley and cream into the pan and leave to bubble for a few minutes until the sauce has thickened slightly. Season to taste with salt and pepper, then pour over the pork and serve immediately.

cook's tip

Veal stock is mellow in flavour and does not overpower other ingredients. It is a mainstay of restaurant kitchens, but is made less frequently at home. If you can't get ready-made fresh veal stock, chicken stock is a satisfactory alternative.

NUTRITIONAL INFORMATION: Energy 375kcal/1563kJ; Protein 28.7g; Carbohydrate 15g, of which sugars 12.7g; Fat 20.5g, of which saturates 11.3g; Cholesterol 118mg; Calcium 58mg; Fibre 2.2g; Sodium 141mg.

Pork Loin with Celery

Have a change from a plain roast and try this loin of pork in an unusual celery and cream sauce.

ingredients

SERVES FOUR

- 15ml/1 tbsp vegetable oil
- 50g/2oz/¼ cup butter
- 1kg/2¼lb boned, rolled loin of pork, rind removed and trimmed
- 1 onion, chopped
- 1 bouquet garni
- 3 fresh dill sprigs
- 150ml/¼ pint/⅔ cup dry white wine
- 150ml/¼ pint/⅔ cup water
- sticks from 1 celery head, cut into 2.5cm/1in lengths
- 25g/1oz/¼ cup plain (all-purpose) flour
- 150ml/¼ pint/⅔ cup double (heavy) cream
- squeeze of lemon juice
- salt and ground black pepper
- chopped fresh dill, to garnish

1 Heat the oil and half the butter in a heavy pan just large enough to hold the pork and celery. Add the pork and cook, turning frequently, for 8–10 minutes, until browned. Transfer the pork to a plate.

2 Add the onion to the pan and cook, stirring occasionally, for 5 minutes, until softened but not coloured.

cook's tip

Pork loin is a lean joint that goes well with creamy sauces.

3 Add the bouquet garni and dill sprigs, place the pork on top and add any accumulated juices from the plate. Pour in the wine and water, season to taste, cover the pan and simmer gently for 30 minutes.

4 Turn the pork over, arrange the celery around it, cover again and cook for 40 minutes, until the pork and celery are tender. Lift out the pork and celery with a slotted spoon and transfer to a serving plate, cover and keep warm. Discard the bouquet garni and dill.

5 Cream the remaining butter with the flour, then whisk into the cooking liquid while it is barely simmering. Cook for 2–3 minutes, stirring occasionally. Stir the cream into the sauce, bring to the boil and add a squeeze of lemon juice.

6 Slice the pork, spoon a little sauce over it and garnish with dill. Serve the remaining sauce separately.

NUTRITIONAL INFORMATION: Energy 669kcal/2783kJ; Protein 55.6g; Carbohydrate 8.1g, of which sugars 3g; Fat 43.5g, of which saturates 22.9g; Cholesterol 236mg; Calcium 105mg; Fibre 1.3g; Sodium 336mg.

Pork with Mustard Sauce

Fry the apple for this dish very carefully, because it will disintegrate if it is overcooked.

ingredients

SERVES FOUR

- 500g/1¼lb pork fillet (tenderloin)
- 1 tart eating apple, such as Granny Smith
- 40g/1½oz/3 tbsp butter
- 15g/½oz/1 tbsp caster (superfine) sugar
- 1 small onion, finely chopped
- 30ml/2 tbsp Calvados or brandy
- 15ml/1 tbsp Meaux or coarse grain mustard
- 15ml/¼ pint/⅔ cup double (heavy) cream
- 30ml/2 tbsp chopped fresh parsley
- salt and ground black pepper

1 Cut the pork fillet into thin even size slices with a sharp knife. Peel and core the apple, then cut it into thick slices.

2 Heat a wok, then add half the butter. When the butter is hot, add the apple slices, sprinkle the sugar over them and fry for 2–3 minutes, stirring constantly, allowing the sugar to caramelize but not burn.

3 Remove the apple slices from the wok and set aside. Wipe out the wok with kitchen paper.

4 Reheat the wok, then add the remaining butter and stir-fry the pork fillet and onion together for approximately 2–3 minutes, until the pork is turning a golden colour and the onion has begun to soften. Do not overcook the pork.

5 Stir in the Calvados or brandy, bring to the boil and cook until it has reduced by about half. Stir the mustard into the sauce, add the cream and simmer gently for about 1 minute, then stir in the chopped parsley. Transfer the pork to warmed plates, divide the apple slices among them and serve immediately.

cook's tip

If you haven't got a wok, use a large frying pan, preferably with deep, sloping sides.

NUTRITIONAL INFORMATION: Energy 278kcal/1162kJ; Protein 27.5g; Carbohydrate 7.8g, of which sugars 7.4g; Fat 15.4g, of which saturates 8.2g; Cholesterol 105mg; Calcium 42mg; Fibre 1.2g; Sodium 154mg.

Pork Satay

These delightful little satay sticks from Thailand are served with spicy peanut sauce.

ingredients

MAKES EIGHT

- ½ small onion, chopped
- 2 garlic cloves, crushed
- 30ml/2 tbsp lemon juice
- 15ml/1 tbsp soy sauce
- 5ml/1 tsp ground coriander
- 2.5ml/½ tsp ground cumin
- 5ml/1 tsp ground turmeric
- 30ml/2 tbsp vegetable oil
- 450g/1lb pork fillet (tenderloin)
- salt and ground black pepper
- fresh coriander (cilantro) sprigs, to garnish
- boiled rice, to serve
- ½ small cucumber, peeled, diced and sprinkled with white wine vinegar, to serve

For the sauce

- 150ml/¼ pint/⅔ cup coconut cream
- 60ml/4 tbsp crunchy peanut butter
- 15ml/1 tbsp lemon juice
- 2.5ml/½ tsp ground cumin
- 2.5ml/½ tsp ground coriander
- 5ml/1 tsp soft brown sugar
- 15ml/1 tbsp soy sauce
- 1–2 dried red chillies, seeded and chopped
- 15ml/1 tbsp chopped fresh coriander

1 Put the onion, garlic, lemon juice, soy sauce, ground coriander, cumin, turmeric and oil in a food processor and process until smooth. Cut the pork into thin strips, mix with the spice marinade in a bowl, cover with clear film (plastic wrap) and chill for 20 minutes.

2 Preheat the grill (broiler). Thread two or three pieces of pork on to each of eight soaked wooden skewers and grill (broil) for 2–3 minutes on each side, basting with the marinade, until cooked through.

3 To make the sauce, put all the ingredients into a pan, bring to the boil, stirring constantly, and simmer for 5 minutes.

4 Arrange the satay sticks on a platter, garnish with coriander sprigs and season. Serve immediately with the peanut sauce, accompanied with boiled rice and diced cucumber.

cook's tip

Serve pork satay sticks as a light meal or first course. They also make irresistible party snacks.

NUTRITIONAL INFORMATION: Energy 189kcal/784kJ; Protein 14.5g; Carbohydrate 2.9g, of which sugars 2.2g; Fat 13.3g, of which saturates 5.8g; Cholesterol 35mg; Calcium 25mg; Fibre 0.9g; Sodium 70mg.

Stir-fried Pork & Lychees

No extra oil or fat is needed to cook this dish, as the pork produces enough on its own.

ingredients

SERVES FOUR

- 450g/1lb fatty pork, such as belly pork, with the skin left on or removed
- 30ml/2 tbsp hoisin sauce
- 4 spring onions (scallions), sliced diagonally
- 175g/6oz lychees, peeled, stoned (pitted) and cut into slivers
- salt and ground black pepper
- whole lychees and fresh parsley sprigs, to garnish

cook's tips

• *Lychees have a very pretty pink skin, which cracks easily when the fruit is pressed between finger and thumb, making them easy to peel. The fruit is a soft, fleshy berry and contains a long, shiny, brown seed. This is inedible and must be removed. The sweet flesh is pearly white and fragrant, similar in texture to a grape.*

• *When buying lychees, avoid any that are turning brown, as they will be over-ripe. Equally, avoid under-ripe lychees with green or beige skins. Look for fruit with as much red or pink in the skins as possible. They should be used as soon after purchase as possible, but can be stored in the refrigerator for up to a week. If you cannot buy the fresh fruit, you could use drained canned lychees, but they do not have the same fragrance or flavour.*

1 Cut the pork into bitesize pieces and place in a dish. Pour the hoisin sauce over the meat and toss well to coat the pieces thoroughly. Cover with clear film (plastic wrap) and leave to marinate in a cool place for at least 30 minutes.

2 Heat a wok over a high heat, then add the pork and stir-fry for 5 minutes, until the fat runs and the meat is crisp and golden and cooked through. Add the spring onions and stir-fry for a further 2 minutes until softened and browned.

3 Sprinkle the lychee slivers over the pork, stir briefly and season the dish well with salt and pepper. Transfer to warmed plates, garnish each plate with two or three whole lychees and fresh parsley sprigs and serve immediately.

NUTRITIONAL INFORMATION: Energy 465kcal/1926kJ; Protein 17.9g; Carbohydrate 8.7g, of which sugars 8.6g; Fat 40.1g, of which saturates 14.8g; Cholesterol 81mg; Calcium 17mg; Fibre 0.5g; Sodium 206mg.

Soufflé Omelette

This delectable fluffy omelette is light and delicate enough to melt in the mouth.

ingredients

SERVES ONE

- 2 eggs, separated
- 30ml/2 tbsp cold water
- 15ml/1 tbsp chopped fresh coriander (cilantro)
- 7.5ml/1½ tsp olive oil
- 30ml/2 tbsp mango chutney
- 25g/1oz/¼ cup grated Jarlsberg cheese
- salt and ground black pepper
- fresh salad, to serve

3 Gently fold the whisked egg whites into the egg yolk mixture with a rubber spatula, keeping as much air in the egg whites as possible.

4 Heat the oil in a small frying pan, pour in the egg mixture and reduce the heat. Do not stir. Cook until the omelette becomes puffy and is golden brown on the underside (lift one edge to check).

5 Spoon the mango chutney over the omelette and sprinkle with the grated cheese. Fold the omelette over and slide on to a warmed plate. Serve while hot, with salad. (If you like, place the pan under a hot grill/broiler to set the top of the omelette before adding the chutney and cheese.)

cook's tip

• If there is any trace of grease – and that includes any yolk – egg whites will not foam when whisked. It's best to use a glass, china or metal bowl. Plastic is easily scratched and then traces of grease are almost impossible to remove. The perfect choice is copper, as the whites react with the metal to create a full and stable foam. However, do not leave them to stand in a copper bowl, as they will turn grey.

• Whatever the material, the bowl you choose should be a generous size to allow plenty of room for whisking.

1 Beat the egg yolks together with the cold water and coriander in a bowl and season with salt and pepper.

2 Whisk the egg whites in another grease-free bowl until stiff peaks form.

NUTRITIONAL INFORMATION: Energy 377kcal/1570kJ; Protein 19g; Carbohydrate 14.9g, of which sugars 14.8g; Fat 27g, of which saturates 9.2g; Cholesterol 405mg; Calcium 249mg; Fibre 0.3g; Sodium 648mg.

Cheese Bubble & Squeak

This London dish was originally made for breakfast with vegetables left over from the previous day.

ingredients

SERVES FOUR

- about 450g/1lb/3 cups mashed potatoes
- about 225g/8oz/4 cups shredded cooked cabbage or kale
- 1 large egg, lightly beaten
- 115g/4oz/1 cup grated Cheddar cheese
- pinch of freshly grated nutmeg
- salt and ground black pepper
- plain (all-purpose) flour, for coating
- vegetable oil, for frying

variation

To make the traditional version of bubble and squeak, heat 30ml/2 tbsp beef dripping (drippings) or vegetable oil in a large frying pan. Add 1 finely chopped onion and cook over low heat, stirring occasionally, for about 5 minutes, until softened but not coloured.

Using a slotted spoon, transfer the cooked onion to a bowl and mix with the other ingredients in step 1, omitting the cheese and using finely chopped cooked cabbage or Brussels sprouts. Use the same frying pan for cooking the patties in step 3.

1 Mix together the mashed potatoes, shredded cooked cabbage or kale, egg, cheese and nutmeg in a bowl and season with salt and pepper. Wit wet hands, shape the mixture into a large flat pattie and place on a plate.

2 Cover with clear film (plastic wrap) and chill in the refrigerator for 1 hour or more, if possible, as this helps firm up the mixture.

3 Gently sprinkle flour over the pattie to coat lightly. Heat about 1cm/¹/₂in oil in a frying pan until it is quite hot. Carefully slide the pattie into the oil and cook for about 8 minutes on each side, until golden and crisp. Remove with a slotted spatula, drain on kitchen paper and serve hot and crisp.

NUTRITIONAL INFORMATION: Energy 281kcal/1175kJ; Protein 11.6g; Carbohydrate 21g, of which sugars 4.3g; Fat 16.7g, of which saturates 7.4g; Cholesterol 75mg; Calcium 254mg; Fibre 2.3g; Sodium 242mg.

Grilled Vegetables on Rice

A warm salad of summer vegetables is served on wild and white rice tossed in a garlicky dressing.

ingredients

SERVES FOUR

- 225g/8oz/1¼ cups wild and long grain rice mixture
- 1 large aubergine (eggplant), thickly sliced
- 1 red, 1 yellow and 1 green (bell) pepper, seeded and cut into quarters
- 2 red onions, sliced
- 225g/8oz brown cap or shiitake mushrooms
- 2 small courgettes (zucchini), cut in half lengthways
- olive oil, for brushing
- 30ml/2 tbsp chopped fresh thyme
- salt and ground black pepper

For the dressing

- 90ml/6 tbsp extra virgin olive oil
- 30ml/2 tbsp balsamic vinegar
- 2 garlic cloves, crushed

1 Put the rice mixture in a pan of cold salted water. Bring to the boil, reduce the heat, cover with a tight-fitting lid and cook gently for 30–40 minutes or according to the packet instructions, until all the grains are tender.

2 To make the salad dressing, mix together the olive oil, vinegar and garlic, adding salt and pepper to taste, in a small bowl or screw-top jar until the ingredients are well blended. Set aside while you cook the vegetables.

3 Arrange the vegetables on a grill (broiler) rack. Brush with olive oil and grill (broil) for 8–10 minutes, until tender and well browned, turning them occasionally and brushing again with oil.

cook's tip

Wild rice is not a rice at all, but is actually a type of wild grass. It has a wonderfully nutty flavour and also adds an attractive contrast of colour and texture when mixed with long grain rice. The two grains are available ready-mixed from supermarkets.

4 When the rice is cooked, drain and toss in half the dressing. Turn it into a serving dish and arrange the grilled vegetables on top. Pour the remaining dressing over the vegetables and sprinkle with chopped fresh thyme. Serve warm.

NUTRITIONAL INFORMATION: Energy 438kcal/1824kJ; Protein 8.6g; Carbohydrate 60.3g, of which sugars 13.6g; Fat 18.1g, of which saturates 2.7g; Cholesterol 0mg; Calcium 56mg; Fibre 5 1g; Sodium 12mg.

Spinach & Avocado Salad

Young spinach leaves are served with avocado, tomatoes and radishes in an unusual tofu sauce.

ingredients

SERVES FOUR TO SIX

- 1 large avocado
- juice of 1 lime
- 225g/8oz/4 cups baby spinach leaves
- 115g/4oz cherry tomatoes
- 4 spring onions (scallions), sliced
- ½ cucumber
- 50g/2oz radishes

For the dressing

- 115g/4oz soft silken tofu
- 45ml/3 tbsp milk
- 10ml/2 tsp mustard
- 2.5ml/½ tsp white wine vinegar
- cayenne pepper
- salt and ground black pepper
- radish roses and fresh herb sprigs, to garnish

1 Cut the avocado in half, remove the stone (pit) and strip off the skin. Cut the flesh into slices. Transfer the slices to a plate, drizzle over the lime juice and set aside.

2 Rinse and thoroughly dry the baby spinach leaves. Put them in a mixing bowl.

3 Cut the larger cherry tomatoes in half and add all the tomatoes to the mixing bowl with the spring onions. Cut the cucumber into even-sized chunks and slice the radishes thinly. Add the cucumber and radishes to the bowl.

4 To make the dressing, put the silken tofu, milk, mustard, wine vinegar and a pinch of cayenne in a food processor or blender. Add salt and pepper to taste, then process for about 30 seconds or until the dressing is smooth.

5 Scrape the dressing into a bowl and add a little extra milk if you like a thinner consistency. Sprinkle with a little extra cayenne and garnish with radish roses and herb sprigs.

6 Arrange the avocado slices with the spinach salad on a serving dish and serve immediately, handing the tofu dressing separately.

cook's tip

Tofu, or beancurd, has a bland flavour and comes in firm and silken forms. The firm variety is also sold fried or smoked.

NUTRITIONAL INFORMATION: Energy 71kcal/293kJ; Protein 2.8g; Carbohydrate 2g, of which sugars 1.6g; Fat 5.7g, of which saturates 1.2g; Cholesterol 0mg; Calcium 135mg; Fibre 1.7g; Sodium 46mg.

Potato & Feta Patties

These delicious fried mouthfuls, flavoured with dill and lemon sauce make a perfect supper dish.

ingredients

SERVES SIX

- 500g/1¼lb floury potatoes
- 115g/4oz/1 cup feta cheese
- 4 spring onions, chopped
- 45ml/3 tbsp chopped fresh dill
- 1 egg, beaten
- 15ml/1 tbsp lemon juice
- plain flour, for dredging
- 45ml/3 tbsp olive oil
- salt and ground black pepper
- dill sprigs, to garnish
- shredded spring onions, to garnish
- lemon wedges, to serve
- crisp green salad leaves, to serve

1 Cook the potatoes, still in their skins, in boiling lightly salted water for approximately 20 minutes, or until soft. Drain and leave to cool slightly, then chop them in half and peel while still warm. Discard the skins.

2 Place the cooked potatoes in a bowl and mash. Crumble the feta cheese into the mashed potatoes and add the spring onions, dill, egg and lemon juice and season with salt and pepper. (Feta cheese is naturally salty, so taste the mixture before you add any additional salt.) Stir well.

3 Cover, place in the refrigerator and chill until firm. Divide the mixture into walnut-size balls, then flatten them into oval rounds. Dredge with flour, shaking off the excess.

4 Heat the oil in a large frying pan and fry the patties in batches until golden brown on both sides. Drain on kitchen paper and garnish with spring onions, dill and lemon wedges. Serve hot with crisp green salad leaves.

variations

- *For a spicier version of this dish add a few flakes of dried chilli to the mixture before frying.*

- *If you prefer, any strong-tasting cheese can be used, such as Stilton, Pecorino or Parmesan.*

NUTRITIONAL INFORMATION: Energy 178kcal/744kJ; Protein 5.8g; Carbohydrate 15.9g, of which sugars 1.6g; Fat 10.6g, of which saturates 3.8g; Cholesterol 45mg; Calcium 85mg; Fibre 1g; Sodium 297mg.

Cheese & Onion Pastries

These attractive red onion and goat's cheese pastries couldn't be easier to make.

ingredients

SERVES FOUR

- 15ml/1 tbsp olive oil
- 450g/1lb/1½ cups red onions, sliced
- 30ml/2 tbsp fresh thyme or 10ml/2 tsp dried
- 15ml/1 tbsp balsamic vinegar
- 425g/15oz packet ready-rolled puff pastry
- 115g/4oz/½ cup goat's cheese, cubed
- 1 egg, beaten
- salt and ground black pepper
- fresh thyme sprigs, to garnish
- mixed green salad leaves, to serve

1 Heat the oil in a large frying pan, add the sliced red onions and fry over a gentle heat for approximately 10 minutes or until softened and golden in colour. Add the thyme, salt, black pepper and balsamic vinegar.

2 Continue to cook over a gentle heat for a further 5 minutes, stirring occasionally to prevent the onions from browning. Remove the pan from the heat and set aside to cool for a few minutes.

3 Preheat the oven to 220°C/425°F/Gas 7. Unroll the pastry and, using a 15cm/6in plate as a guide, cut four rounds. Place the pastry rounds on a dampened baking sheet and, using the point of a knife, score a border, 2cm/½in inside the edge of each round.

4 Divide the onions among the pastry rounds and top with the goat's cheese. Brush the edge of each round with beaten egg and bake for 25–30 minutes until golden. Garnish with thyme sprigs, if using, before serving with crisp green salad leaves.

variations

• *You can use French onions if you prefer, but red onions tend to have a more distinctive taste.*

• *Add extra taste by spreading the pastry with pesto or tapenade before adding the filling.*

NUTRITIONAL INFORMATION: Energy 554kcal/2308kJ; Protein 13.5g; Carbohydrate 48.5g, of which sugars 8g; Fat 36.4g, of which saturates 5.6g; Cholesterol 27mg; Calcium 128mg; Fibre 1.6g; Sodium 506mg.

Tofu & Crunchy Vegetables

High protein tofu is nicest if it is marinated lightly before it is cooked.

ingredients

SERVES FOUR

- 2 x 225g/8oz packets smoked tofu, diced
- 45ml/3 tbsp soy sauce
- 30ml/2 tbsp dry sherry or vermouth
- 15ml/1 tbsp sesame oil
- 45ml/3 tbsp groundnut (peanut) or sunflower oil
- 2 red (bell) peppers, seeded and thinly sliced
- 200g/7oz/1⅓ cups mangetouts (snow peas), trimmed and sliced
- 115g/4oz baby corn, halved
- 15ml/1 tbsp sesame seeds
- 2.5ml/½ tsp dried chilli flakes
- small bunch coriander (cilantro), chopped

1 Place the tofu in a shallow dish. Mix together the soy sauce, sherry or vermouth and sesame oil and pour over the tofu. Cover with clear film (plastic wrap) and leave to marinate in a cool place for at least 30 minutes. Drain the tofu cubes and reserve the marinade.

cook's tip

The actual cooking of this dish takes only a few minutes and needs constant attention, so you should have all the ingredients prepared and sliced before you start to heat the wok.

2 Heat a wok or large, heavy frying pan and add the groundnut oil. When the oil is hot, add the cubes of tofu and stir-fry until they are browned all over. Remove the tofu from the pan with a slotted spoon and reserve on a plate.

3 Add the red peppers, mangetouts and baby corn to the pan and stir-fry over a medium heat for approximately 2 minutes.

4 Return the tofu to the pan and pour in the reserved marinade. Heat, stirring gently for a few minutes, until bubbling, then sprinkle with the sesame seeds. Add the chilli flakes and chopped coriander, toss to mix well and serve while still hot.

NUTRITIONAL INFORMATION: Energy 258kcal/1068kJ; Protein 13.5g; Carbohydrate 9.9g, of which sugars 8.5g; Fat 18.4g, of which saturates 2.4g; Cholesterol 0mg; Calcium 626mg; Fibre 3.3g; Sodium 1050mg.

Spicy Quorn with Leeks

Quorn easily absorbs different flavours and retains a good firm texture, making it ideal for stir-frying.

ingredients

SERVES FOUR

- 225g/8oz packet Quorn, diced
- 45ml/3 tbsp dark soy sauce
- 30ml/2 tbsp dry sherry or vermouth
- 10ml/2 tsp clear honey
- 150ml/¼ pint/⅔ cup vegetable stock
- 10ml/2 tsp cornflour (cornstarch)
- 45ml/3 tbsp sunflower or groundnut (peanut) oil
- 3 leeks, thinly sliced
- 1 red chilli, seeded and thinly sliced
- 2.5cm/1in piece fresh root ginger, shredded
- salt and ground black pepper
- rice or egg noodles, to serve

1 Toss the pieces of Quorn in the soy sauce and sherry or vermouth in a bowl. Leave to marinate for 30 minutes.

2 Drain the Quorn and reserve the marinade. Add a little stock to the cornflour to make a paste. Mix the paste with the marinade, the honey and the rest of the stock. Reserve.

3 Heat the oil in a wok or large frying pan and, when hot, add the Quorn and stir-fry until it is crisp on the outside. Remove and set aside.

4 Reheat the oil remaining in the wok. Add the thinly sliced leeks, chilli and ginger and stir-fry for about 2 minutes, until the vegetables are just soft and beginning to brown at the edges. Season to taste with salt and pepper.

5 Return the Quorn to the pan, together with the marinade mixture, and stir well until thick and glossy. Serve immediately with rice or egg noodles.

cook's tip

Quorn is a versatile mycoprotein food, which is available in most supermarkets both as an ingredient and in a range of prepared meals. If you cannot find it, you could use firm tofu for this dish.

NUTRITIONAL INFORMATION: Energy 158kcal/657kJ; Protein 8.6g; Carbohydrate 5.1g, of which sugars 3.8g; Fat 10.6g, of which saturates 1.4g; Cholesterol 0mg; Calcium 27mg; Fibre 4.9g; Sodium 939mg.

Mixed Vegetable Stir-fry

This colourful stir-fried vegetable mixture is coated in a classic Chinese black bean sauce.

ingredients

SERVES FOUR

- 8 spring onions (scallions)
- 225g/8oz button (white) mushrooms
- 1 red (bell) pepper
- 1 green (bell) pepper
- 2 large carrots
- 60ml/4 tbsp groundnut (peanut) or sunflower oil
- 2 garlic cloves, crushed
- 60ml/4 tbsp black bean sauce
- 90ml/6 tbsp warm water
- 225g/8oz/scant 3 cups beansprouts
- salt and ground black pepper

1 Thinly slice the spring onions diagonally and and slice the button mushrooms. Set aside in separate bowls.

2 Cut the red and green peppers in half, remove and discard the seeds and slice the flesh into thin strips.

3 Cut the carrots in half, or in three if they are very long. Cut each half into thin strips lengthways. Stack the slices and cut through them in the same direction to make very fine, even strips.

4 Heat the oil in a large wok or frying pan until very hot. Add the spring onions and garlic and stir-fry for 30 seconds. Add the mushrooms, peppers and carrots. Stir-fry over high heat for a further 5–6 minutes, until just beginning to soften.

5 Mix the black bean sauce with the water. Add to the wok or frying pan and cook for a further 3–4 minutes.

6 Stir in the beansprouts and stir-fry for a final 1 minute, until all the vegetables are coated in the black bean sauce. Season to taste with salt and pepper. Serve immediately.

cook's tip

Black bean sauce is available in jars. Once opened it should be stored in the refrigerator.

NUTRITIONAL INFORMATION: Energy 196kcal/817kJ; Protein 6.5g; Carbohydrate 16.1g, of which sugars 9.4g; Fat 12.2g, of which saturates 1.9g; Cholesterol 0mg; Calcium 45mg; Fibre 4.3g; Sodium 19mg.

Potato & Broccoli Stir-fry

This wonderful stir-fry combines potato, broccoli and red pepper with just a hint of fresh ginger.

ingredients

SERVES TWO

- 450g/1lb potatoes
- 45ml/3 tbsp groundnut (peanut) oil
- 50g/2oz/4 tbsp butter
- 1 small onion, chopped
- 1 red (bell) pepper, seeded and chopped
- 225g/8oz broccoli, broken into florets
- 2.5cm/1in piece of fresh root ginger, grated
- salt and ground black pepper

1 Peel the potatoes and cut them into 1cm/$\frac{1}{2}$in dice. Heat the oil in a wok or a large frying pan. Add the potatoes and cook over a high heat, stirring and tossing frequently, for about 8 minutes, until they are browned and just tender.

cook's tip

Always use a vegetable peeler with a swivel blade for peeling potatoes. As most of the nutrients are directly beneath the skin, it is important to peel them thinly. Alternatively, leave the skins on the potatoes.

2 Drain off the oil from the pan, leaving the potatoes in it. Add the butter to the potatoes in the pan. As soon as it melts and starts to foam, add the chopped onion and red pepper and stir-fry the vegetables for 2 minutes.

3 Add the broccoli florets and ginger to the pan. Over a medium heat, stir-fry for a further 2–3 minutes, taking care not to break up the potatoes. Season to taste with salt and freshly ground black pepper and serve immediately.

variations

• *Substitute 1 finely chopped celery stick and 1 thinly sliced carrot for the red (bell) pepper.*

• *For a milder tasting dish, omit the ginger, replace the broccoli with peeled, seeded and diced tomatoes and flavour with torn fresh basil leaves.*

NUTRITIONAL INFORMATION: Energy 242kcal/1069kJ; Protein 10.2g; Carbohydrate 46.4g, of which sugars 11.8g; Fat 247.4g, of which saturates 55.9g; Cholesterol 53mg; Calcium 96mg; Fibre 7g; Sodium 190mg.

Pepper & Potato Tortilla

A traditional Spanish dish, tortilla is best eaten cold in chunky wedges and is ideal picnic food.

ingredients

SERVES FOUR

- 2 potatoes
- 45ml/3 tbsp olive oil
- 1 large onion, thinly sliced
- 2 garlic cloves, crushed
- 1 green (bell) pepper, seeded and thinly sliced
- 1 red (bell) pepper, seeded and thinly sliced
- 6 eggs, beaten
- 115g/4oz/1 cup grated mature (sharp) Cheddar or Mahón cheese
- salt and ground black pepper

1 Do not peel the potatoes, but scrub the skins well under cold running water. Par-boil them for about 10 minutes, then drain and, when they are cool enough to handle, slice them thickly. Preheat the grill (broiler).

2 Heat the oil in a large non-stick or well seasoned frying pan. Add the onion, garlic and green and red peppers and cook over medium heat, stirring occasionally, for about 5 minutes, until softened but not coloured.

3 Add the potatoes to the pan, lower the heat and cook very gently, stirring occasionally to prevent the vegetables sticking, until the potatoes are completely cooked and the other vegetables are soft. Add a little extra olive oil if the pan seems too dry.

4 Pour half the beaten eggs into the pan around the vegetables, then sprinkle over half the grated cheese. Add the rest of the eggs. Season with salt and pepper and sprinkle with the remaining cheese.

5 Continue to cook over low heat, without stirring, half covering the pan with a lid to help set the eggs.

6 When the mixture is firm, place the pan under the hot grill for a few seconds to seal the top lightly. Leave the tortilla in the pan to cool. This helps it firm up further and makes it easier to turn out. Cut into generous wedges or squares and serve at room temperature.

variation

For a more basic, rustic, tortilla, omit the peppers, garlic and cheese and replace with larger amounts of potato and onion.

NUTRITIONAL INFORMATION: Energy 321kcal/1333kJ; Protein 13.1g; Carbohydrate 19.6g, of which sugars 10.2g; Fat 21.1g, of which saturates 8.3g; Cholesterol 123mg; Calcium 256mg; Fibre 3g; Sodium 254mg.

Onion & Gruyère Tart

The secret of this tart is to cook the onions very slowly until they almost caramelize.

ingredients

SERVES FOUR

- 175g/6oz/1½ cups plain (all-purpose) flour
- pinch of salt
- 75g/3oz/6 tbsp butter, diced
- 1 egg yolk

For the filling

- 50g/2oz/4 tbsp butter
- 450g/1lb onions, thinly sliced
- 15ml/1 tbsp wholegrain mustard
- 2 eggs, plus 1 egg yolk
- 300ml/½ pint/1 cup double (heavy) cream
- 75g/3oz/¾ cup grated Gruyère cheese
- pinch of freshly grated nutmeg
- salt and ground black pepper

1 Sift the flour and salt into a bowl. Add the butter and rub it into the flour until the mixture resembles fine breadcrumbs. Add the egg yolk and 15ml/1 tbsp cold water and mix to a firm dough. Chill for 30 minutes.

2 Preheat the oven to 200°C/400°F/Gas 6. Knead the dough, then roll it out and use to line a 23cm/9in loose-based flan tin (pan). Prick the base all over with a fork, line the pastry case (pie shell) with baking parchment and fill with baking beans.

3 Bake the pastry case blind for 15 minutes. Remove the paper and beans and bake for a further 10–15 minutes, until the pastry case is crisp. Meanwhile, melt the butter in a pan, add the onions, cover with a tight-fitting lid and cook over low heat, stirring occasionally, for 20 minutes, until golden.

cook's tip

Leave pastry to rest for at least 30 minutes before rolling out, chilling it in the refrigerator, to stop it shrinking during baking.

4 Reduce the oven temperature to 180°C/350°F/Gas 4. Spread the pastry case with mustard and top with the onions.

5 Mix together the eggs, egg yolk, cream, cheese and nutmeg and season with salt and pepper. Pour over the onions. Bake for 30–35 minutes, until golden. Remove the tart from the oven and leave to cool slightly. Serve warm.

NUTRITIONAL INFORMATION: Energy 904kcal/3746kJ; Protein 15g; Carbohydrate 36.7g, of which sugars 3g; Fat 78.2g, of which saturates 47g; Cholesterol 384mg; Calcium 272mg; Fibre 1.6g; Sodium 383mg.

Green Vegetable Pasta

A wonderful medley of vegetables, tossed in fresh pasta and bursting with fresh flavours.

ingredients

SERVES FOUR

- 2 carrots
- 1 courgette (zucchini)
- 75g/3oz French (green) beans
- 1 small leek
- 1 handful fresh flat-leaf parsley
- 2 ripe Italian plum tomatoes
- 25g/1oz/2 tbsp butter
- 45ml/3 tbsp olive oil
- 2.5ml/½ tsp sugar
- 115g/4oz/1 cup frozen peas
- salt and ground black pepper
- 350g/12oz/3 cups dried penne pasta
- freshly grated Parmesan cheese, to serve

1 Dice the carrots and the courgette finely. Top and tail the French beans, then cut them into 2cm/3⁄4in lengths. Slice the leek thinly. Peel and dice the tomatoes. Chop the flat-leaf parsley and set all the ingredients aside.

2 Melt the butter in the oil in a medium frying pan or heavy pan. When the mixture begins to sizzle, quickly add the prepared leek and carrots. Sprinkle the sugar over and fry, stirring frequently, for approximately 5 minutes.

3 Stir in the courgette, French beans, peas and plenty of salt and pepper. Cover and cook gently over a low to medium heat for approximately 5–8 minutes or until the vegetables are tender, stirring occasionally to keep them from burning.

4 Meanwhile, bring a pan of water to the boil and cook the penne until *al dente*.

5 Stir in the parsley and tomatoes and adjust the seasoning. Serve immediately, with the penne and grated Parmesan cheese.

NUTRITIONAL INFORMATION: Energy 400kcal/1692kJ; Protein 15.3g; Carbohydrate 76.9g, of which sugars 11.7g; Fat 5.6g, of which saturates 0.9g; Cholesterol 0mg; Calcium 76mg; Fibre 7.2g; Sodium 21mg.

Spaghetti with Herbs

Fresh herbs make a wonderful aromatic sauce – the heat from the pasta releases their flavour.

cook's tip

• *When cooking long strands of pasta such as spaghetti, gather into a bunch and drop one end into the boiling water. As the pasta softens, push it down gently until it bends in the middle and is completely immersed.*

• *Refer to the packet instructions for cooking times as these can vary. As a general rule, dried pasta needs 8–10 minutes. Do not be tempted to overcook pasta; it should be "al dente", that is, tender but still firm to the bite. Always test pasta just before you think it should be ready.*

1 Bring a large pan of lightly salted water to the boil and add the spaghetti, cooking it over a medium heat for about 10 minutes.

2 With a sharp knife, chop the fresh herbs roughly or finely, whichever you prefer.

3 When the pasta is almost *al dente*, melt the butter in a large frying pan or heavy pan. As soon as the butter begins to sizzle, drain the spaghetti and add it to the pan, then sprinkle in the chopped herbs and salt and pepper to taste.

4 Toss over a medium heat until the pasta is completely coated in the oil and herbs. Serve immediately in bowls, sprinkled with extra herb leaves and flowers. Hand around freshly grated Parmesan cheese separately.

Rocket & Tomato Pizza

Peppery rocket leaves and aromatic basil add colour and flavour to this pizza.

ingredients

SERVES TWO

- 10ml/2 tsp olive oil, plus extra for oiling and drizzling
- 1 garlic clove, crushed
- 150g/5oz/1 cup canned chopped tomatoes
- 2.5ml/½ tsp sugar
- 30ml/2 tbsp torn basil leaves
- 2 tomatoes, seeded and chopped
- 150g/5oz/⅔ cup mozzarella cheese, sliced
- 20g/¾oz/1 cup rocket leaves
- rock salt and ground black pepper

For the pizza base

- 225g/8oz/2 cups strong white bread flour, sifted
- 5ml/1 tsp salt
- 2.5ml/½ tsp easy-blend (rapid-rise) dried yeast
- 15ml/1 tbsp olive oil
- 150ml/¼ pint/⅔ cup warm water

1 To make the pizza base, mix the flour, salt and yeast in a bowl. Make a well in the centre and add the oil and warm water. Mix to form a soft dough.

2 Turn out the dough on to a lightly floured work surface and knead for 5 minutes. Cover and leave to rest for 5 minutes, then knead for another 5 minutes until the dough is smooth and elastic. Place in a lightly oiled bowl and cover with clear film (plastic wrap). Leave in a warm place for about 45 minutes until doubled in size.

3 Preheat the oven to 220°C/425°F/Gas 7. To make the topping, heat the oil in a frying pan and fry the garlic for 1 minute. Add the canned tomatoes and sugar and cook for 5–7 minutes until reduced and thickened. Stir in the basil and season to taste with salt and pepper. Set aside.

4 Knead the risen dough lightly, then roll out to form a rough 30cm/12in round. Place on an oiled baking sheet and push up the edges of the dough to form a shallow, even rim.

5 Spoon the tomato mixture over the pizza base, then top with the fresh tomatoes and mozzarella. Adjust the seasoning and drizzle with a little olive oil. Bake for 10–12 minutes until crisp and golden. Arrange the rocket over the pizza just before serving.

NUTRITIONAL INFORMATION: Energy 735kcal/3087kJ; Protein 26.1g; Carbohydrate 93g, of which sugars 7.3g; Fat 31.3g, of which saturates 12.7g; Cholesterol 44mg; Calcium 459mg; Fibre 5.5g; Sodium 330mg.

Wild Rice Pilaff

Wild rice has a wonderful nutty flavour and combines well with long grain rice in this fruity mixture.

ingredients

SERVES SIX

- 200g/7oz/1 cup wild rice
- 40g/1½oz/3 tbsp butter
- ½ onion, finely chopped
- 200g/7oz/1 cup long grain rice
- 475ml/16fl oz/2 cups chicken stock
- 75g/3oz/¾ cup flaked almonds
- 115g/4oz/½ cup sultanas (golden raisins)
- 30ml/2 tbsp chopped parsley
- salt and ground black pepper

3 Stir in the stock and bring to the boil. Cover and simmer gently for 30–40 minutes, until the liquid has been absorbed.

1 Bring a large pan of water to the boil. Add the wild rice and 5ml/1 tsp salt. Lower the heat, cover and simmer gently for around 45–60 minutes, until the rice is tender. Drain the rice well.

cook's tip

If you don't have access to a wok it is still possible to stir-fry in a large frying pan which has fairly deep sides. However, in a flat-bottomed pan the heat will be less evenly distributed and it is harder to toss the ingredients cleanly.

2 Meanwhile, melt 15g/½oz/ 1 tbsp of the butter in another pan. Add the onion and cook over a medium heat for about 5 minutes, stirring constantly, until it is just softened. Stir in the long grain rice and cook for a further minute.

4 Melt the remaining butter in a pan. Add the almonds and cook until just golden. Put the rice mixture in a bowl and add the almonds, sultanas and parsley. Stir to mix. Transfer to a warmed serving dish, add the parsley and serve.

NUTRITIONAL INFORMATION: Energy 424kcal/1769kJ; Protein 8.4g; Carbohydrate 68.3g, of which sugars 14.6g; Fat 13g, of which saturates 4g; Cholesterol 14mg; Calcium 69mg; Fibre 1.7g; Sodium 48mg.

Fruity Brown Rice

An oriental-style dressing gives this colourful rice salad extra piquancy.

ingredients

SERVES FOUR

- 115g/4oz/⅔ cup brown rice
- 1 small red (bell) pepper, seeded and diced
- 200g/7oz can corn kernels, drained
- 45ml/3 tbsp sultanas (golden raisins)
- 225g/8oz can pineapple pieces in fruit juice
- 15ml/1 tbsp light soy sauce
- 15ml/1 tbsp sunflower oil
- 15ml/1 tbsp hazelnut oil
- 1 garlic clove, crushed
- 5ml/1 tsp finely chopped fresh root ginger
- salt and ground black pepper
- 4 spring onions (scallions), diagonally sliced, to garnish

1 Bring a large pan of lightly salted water to the boil and cook the brown rice for about 30 minutes, or until it is just tender. Drain thoroughly, rinse under cold water and drain again. Set aside to cool.

cook's tip

• *Hazelnut oil has a distinctive flavour and like olive oil contains mainly mono-unsaturated fats.*

• *Brown rice is not the whole grain: the outer husk is inedible and is removed from all rice, but the bran is left on brown rice.*

2 When the rice is cold, turn it into a large serving bowl and add the diced red pepper, corn kernels and sultanas. Drain the pineapple pieces, reserving the fruit juice, then add them to the rice mixture and toss together lightly.

3 Pour the reserved fruit juice into a clean screw-top jar. Add the soy sauce, sunflower and hazelnut oils, garlic and chopped root ginger. Season to taste with salt and pepper. Close the jar tightly and shake vigorously to combine.

4 Pour the dressing over the salad and toss well. Scatter the spring onions over the top and serve.

NUTRITIONAL INFORMATION: Energy 189kcal/797kJ; Protein 3g; Carbohydrate 35.5g, of which sugars 14.4g; Fat 4.8g, of which saturates 0.6g; Cholesterol 0mg; Calcium 18mg; Fibre 1.9g; Sodium 272mg.

Aubergine Pilaff

This hearty dish made with bulgur wheat is perfect for a midweek supper as it is quick to prepare.

ingredients

SERVES TWO

- 2 aubergines (eggplants)
- 60–90ml/4–6 tbsp sunflower oil
- 1 small onion, finely chopped
- 175g/6oz/1 cup bulgur wheat
- 450ml/¾ pint/scant 2 cups vegetable stock
- 30ml/2 tbsp pine nuts, toasted
- 15ml/1 tbsp chopped fresh mint
- salt and ground black pepper

For the garnish

- lime wedges
- lemon wedges
- fresh mint sprigs

1 Trim the ends from the aubergines, then slice them lengthways. Cut each slice into neat sticks and then into 1cm/½in dice.

2 Heat 60ml/4 tbsp of the oil in a large, heavy frying pan, add the chopped onion and fry over medium heat for 1 minute until beginning to soften. Add the diced aubergine. Increase the heat to high and cook, stirring frequently, for about 4 minutes until the vegetables are just tender. Add the remaining oil if needed.

3 Stir in the bulgur wheat, mixing well to coat it with oil, then pour in the vegetable stock. Bring to the boil, then lower the heat and simmer for 10 minutes or until all the liquid has been absorbed. Season to taste with salt and pepper.

4 Stir in the pine nuts and mint, then spoon the pilaff on to individual plates. Garnish each portion with lime and lemon wedges. Sprinkle with torn mint leaves for extra colour and serve immediately.

variations

- Use courgettes (zucchini) instead of aubergines, or for something completely different, substitute diced pumpkin or acorn squash.

- Serve the pilaff to accompany grilled or roast lamb.

NUTRITIONAL INFORMATION: Energy 542kcal/2248kJ; Protein 9.6g; Carbohydrate 52.2g, of which sugars 5.3g; Fat 34g, of which saturates 3.5g; Cholesterol 0mg; Calcium 83mg; Fibre 3.7g; Sodium 7mg.

Pear & Cinnamon Fritters

Fritters are a delicious way of persuading children to eat more fruit.

ingredients

SERVES FOUR

- 3 ripe, firm pears
- 30ml/2 tbsp caster (superfine) sugar
- 30ml/2 tbsp Kirsch
- groundnut oil, for frying
- 50g/2oz/1 cup amaretti, finely crushed
- 30ml/2 tbsp caster sugar, to decorate
- 1.5ml/¼ tsp ground cinnamon, to decorate
- clotted cream, to serve

For the batter

- 75g/3oz/¾ cup plain (all-purpose) flour
- 1.5ml/¼ tsp salt
- 1.5ml/¼ tsp ground cinnamon
- 60ml/4 tbsp milk
- 2 eggs, separated
- 45ml/3 tbsp water

1 Peel the pears, cut them in quarters and remove the cores. Toss the wedges in the caster sugar and Kirsch. Set aside for 15 minutes.

2 Make the batter. Sift the flour, salt and cinnamon into a large bowl. Beat in the milk, egg yolks and water until smooth. Set aside for 10 minutes.

3 Whisk the egg whites in a grease-free bowl until they form stiff peaks easily; lightly fold them into the cinnamon batter.

4 Preheat the oven to 150°C/300°F/Gas 2. Pour oil into a deep heavy pan to a depth of 7.5cm/3in. Heat to 185°C/360°F or until a bread cube, added to the oil, browns in 45 seconds.

5 Toss a pear wedge in the amaretti crumbs, then spear it on a fork and dip it into the batter until evenly coated. Lower it gently into the hot oil and use a knife to push it off the fork. Add more wedges in the same way but do not overfill the pan.

6 Cook the fritters for 3–4 minutes or until crisp and golden all over. Drain on kitchen paper. Keep in the oven while cooking successive batches. Mix the sugar and cinnamon and sprinkle some over the fritters. Sprinkle a little cinnamon sugar over the clotted cream; serve with the hot fritters.

NUTRITIONAL INFORMATION: Energy 281kcal/1179kJ; Protein 5.8g; Carbohydrate 39.5g, of which sugars 25.2g; Fat 11.6g, of which saturates 1.9g; Cholesterol 96mg; Calcium 77mg; Fibre 3.1g; Sodium 194mg.

Sticky Toffee Pudding

Filling, warming and packed with calories, this gooey steamed pudding is a firm favourite.

ingredients

SERVES SIX

- 115g/4oz/1 cup toasted walnuts, chopped
- 175g/6oz/¾ cup butter, plus extra for greasing
- 175g/6oz/1 cup soft, dark brown sugar
- 60ml/4 tbsp double (heavy) cream
- 30ml/2 tbsp lemon juice
- 2 eggs, beaten
- 115g/4oz/1 cup self-raising (self-rising) flour

1 Grease a 900ml/1½ pint/3¾ cup heatproof deep pudding bowl and add half the chopped walnuts.

2 To make the sticky toffee topping and sauce for the pudding, heat 50g/2oz/¼ cup of the butter with 50g/2oz/¼ cup of the sugar, the cream and 15ml/1 tbsp of the lemon juice in a small pan, stirring until smooth. Pour half into the greased bowl, then swirl to coat it a little way up the sides. Reserve the rest of the sauce for serving.

3 Beat the remaining butter and sugar until light and fluffy, then gradually beat in the eggs. Fold in the flour and the remaining nuts and lemon juice and spoon into the bowl.

4 Cover the bowl with baking parchment with a pleat folded in the centre, then tie securely with string.

cook's tip

Always use boiling water if you need to top up the water in the pan while steaming the pudding.

5 Place the pudding bowl in a large pan with enough water to come halfway up the sides of the bowl. Cover the pan with a lid and bring the water to the boil. Keep the water boiling gently and steam the pudding for 1¼ hours, topping up the water as required, until the pudding is completely set in the centre. Alternatively, steam the pudding in a steamer.

6 Just before serving, gently warm the reserved sticky toffee sauce. To serve, run a knife around the edge of the pudding to loosen it, then put a warm plate over the bowl and turn the pudding out. Pour the warm sauce over it and serve immediately.

NUTRITIONAL INFORMATION: Energy 603kcal/2510kJ; Protein 7.2g; Carbohydrate 46.4g, of which sugars 31.6g; Fat 44.6g, of which saturates 20.2g; Cholesterol 139mg; Calcium 80mg; Fibre 1.3g; Sodium 206mg.

Crêpes Suzette

This dish is a classic of French cuisine and still enjoys worldwide popularity.

ingredients

MAKES EIGHT

- 115g/4oz/1 cup plain (all-purpose) flour
- pinch of salt
- 1 egg
- 1 egg yolk
- 300ml/½ pint/1¼ cups milk
- 15g/½ oz/1 tbsp butter, melted, plus extra for frying

For the sauce

- 2 large oranges
- 50g/2oz/¼ cup butter
- 50g/2oz/¼ cup soft light brown sugar
- 15ml/1 tbsp Grand Marnier
- 15ml/1 tbsp brandy

1 Sift the flour and salt into a bowl and make a well in the centre. Crack the egg and extra yolk into the well. Stir the eggs to incorporate all the flour. When the mixture thickens, gradually add the milk, beating well after each addition, to form a batter. Stir in the butter, transfer to a jug (pitcher), cover and chill for 30 minutes.

cook's tip

Crêpes Suzette are traditionally flambéed at the table in a chafing dish, to spectacular effect.

2 Heat a shallow frying pan, add a little butter and melt until sizzling. Pour in a little batter, tilting the pan so that it just covers the base. Cook over medium heat for 1–2 minutes until the crêpe is lightly browned underneath, then flip and cook for a further minute. Make seven more crêpes in the same way, stacking them on a plate as they are done.

3 Pare the rind from one of the oranges and reserve about 5ml/1 tsp. Squeeze the juice from both oranges.

4 To make the sauce, melt the butter in a large frying pan and heat the sugar with the orange rind and juice until dissolved and gently bubbling. Fold each crêpe in half. Add to the pan one at a time, coat in the sauce and fold in half again. Move to the side of the pan to make room for the others.

5 Pour on the Grand Marnier and brandy and cook gently for 2–3 minutes, until the sauce caramelizes slightly. Sprinkle with the reserved orange rind and serve at once.

NUTRITIONAL INFORMATION: Energy 195kcal/818kJ; Protein 4.4g; Carbohydrate 23.8g, of which sugars 12.8g; Fat 8.9g, of which saturates 5.1g; Cholesterol 69mg; Calcium 100mg; Fibre 1.3g; Sodium 79mg.

Apple Strudel

This Austrian dessert is traditionally made with strudel pastry, but ready-made filo pastry works well.

ingredients

SERVES FOUR TO SIX

- 75g/3oz/¾ cup hazelnuts, chopped and roasted
- 30ml/2 tbsp nibbed almonds, roasted
- 50g/2oz/4 tbsp demerara (raw) sugar
- 2.5ml/½ tsp ground cinnamon
- grated rind and juice of ½ lemon
- 2 large cooking apples, peeled, cored and chopped
- 50g/2oz/⅓ cup sultanas (golden raisins)
- 4 large sheets filo pastry
- 50g/2oz/4 tbsp unsalted (sweet) butter, melted
- sifted icing (confectioners') sugar, for dusting
- cream, custard or yogurt, to serve

1 Preheat the oven to 190°C/375°F/Gas 5. To make the filling, mix together in a bowl the chopped hazelnuts, almonds, sugar, cinnamon, lemon rind and juice, chopped apples and sultanas. Set aside.

2 Spread out one sheet of filo pastry on a clean dish towel and brush the surface with melted butter. Lay a second sheet of filo pastry on top and brush again with melted butter. Repeat with the remaining two sheets, brushing carefully to the edges of the pastry.

3 Spread the fruit and nut mixture over the pastry, leaving a 7.5cm/3in border at each of the shorter ends. Fold the pastry ends in over the filling. Roll up from one long edge to the other, using the dish towel to help support the roll.

cook's tip

Chilled or frozen packs of filo pastry sheets are available from most supermarkets. Work quickly with the thin pastry as it dries out rapidly. Keep the sheets moist under a damp cloth until you are ready to brush them with butter.

4 Carefully transfer the strudel to a greased baking sheet, placing it seam-side down. Brush all over the surface of the pastry with melted butter and bake for 30–35 minutes until golden and crisp.

5 Dust the strudel generously with icing sugar and serve while still hot with cream, custard or yogurt.

NUTRITIONAL INFORMATION: Energy 298kcal/1247kJ; Protein 4.8g; Carbohydrate 31.6g, of which sugars 18.5g; Fat 17.9g, of which saturates 5.2g; Cholesterol 18mg; Calcium 66mg; Fibre 2.4g; Sodium 55mg.

Fruit & Nut Crumble

The classic combination of apples and blackberries is topped with a golden, sweet crumble.

ingredients

SERVES FOUR

- 900g/2lb (about 4 medium) cooking apples, peeled, cored and sliced
- 115g/4oz/½ cup butter, diced, plus extra for greasing
- 115g/4oz/½ cup soft light brown sugar
- 175g/6oz/1½ cups blackberries
- 75g/3oz/¾ cup wholemeal (whole-wheat) flour
- 75g/3oz/¾ cup plain (all-purpose) flour
- 2.5ml/½ tsp ground cinnamon
- 45ml/3 tbsp chopped mixed nuts, toasted

1 Preheat the oven to 180°C/350°F/Gas 4. Lightly butter a 1.2 litre/2 pint/5 cup ovenproof dish.

2 Place the sliced apples in a pan with 25g/1oz/2 tbsp of the butter, 25g/1oz/2 tbsp of the sugar and 15ml/1 tbsp water. Cover the pan with a tight-fitting lid and bring to a simmer over low heat. Cook gently for about 10 minutes, until the apple slices are just tender but are still holding their shape. Remove the pan from the heat.

3 Gently stir in the blackberries and spoon the mixture into the ovenproof dish. Set aside while you make the topping.

4 To make the crumble topping, sift the flours and cinnamon into a bowl, tipping in any of the bran left in the sieve (strainer). Add the remaining 75g/3oz/6 tbsp butter and rub into the flour with your fingertips until the mixture resembles fine breadcrumbs. Alternatively, you can use a food processor to do this stage for you.

5 Stir in the remaining sugar and the nuts and mix well. Sprinkle the crumble topping over the fruit.

6 Bake the crumble for 35–40 minutes until the top is golden brown and the fruit is bubbling. Serve immediately.

cook's tips

• *Try this nut crumble with other fruits such as plums or apricots.*

• *All fruit crumbles are delicious served with cream, ice cream, custard or natural yogurt.*

NUTRITIONAL INFORMATION: Energy 573kcal/2398kJ; Protein 6.8g; Carbohydrate 68.3g, of which sugars 42.3g; Fat 32.2g, of which saturates 15.7g; Cholesterol 61mg; Calcium 86mg; Fibre 5.6g; Sodium 181mg.

Blueberry Pie

This traditional American fruit pie is delicious served cold or warm.

ingredients

SERVES FOUR

- 225g/8oz/2 cups plain (all-purpose) flour
- pinch of salt
- 50g/2oz/¼ cup lard (shortening), diced
- 50g/2oz/¼ cup butter, diced
- 800g/1¾lb/7 cups blueberries
- 25g/1oz/2 tbsp caster (superfine) sugar, plus extra for sprinkling
- 15ml/1 tbsp arrowroot
- 2.5ml/½ tsp ground cinnamon
- grated rind of ½ unwaxed lemon
- beaten egg, to glaze
- crème fraîche, to serve (optional)

1 Sift the flour and salt into a bowl. Rub in the fats with your fingertips until the mixture resembles fine breadcrumbs. Add as much as you need of 45ml/3 tbsp cold water to make a dough that just holds together. Chill for 30 minutes.

2 Place 225g/8oz/2 cups of the blueberries in a pan with the sugar. Cover with a lid and cook gently until the blueberries have softened. Press through a nylon sieve (strainer). Return the puréed blueberries to the pan.

3 Blend the arrowroot with 30ml/2 tbsp cold water and add to the blueberries in the pan. Bring to the boil, stirring until thickened. Allow to cool slightly.

4 Preheat the oven to 190°C/375°F/Gas 5 with a baking sheet inside. Roll out just over half the pastry on a lightly floured surface and use to line a 20cm/8in shallow pie dish.

cook's tip

Cooking the pie on a hot baking sheet helps to crisp the base.

5 Mix together the remaining blueberries, ground cinnamon and lemon rind and spoon into the dish. Pour over the blueberry purée.

6 Use the remaining pastry to cover the pie. Make a slit in the centre. Brush with egg and sprinkle with caster sugar. Bake on the baking sheet for 40–45 minutes. Serve with crème fraîche, if you wish.

NUTRITIONAL INFORMATION: Energy 493kcal/2063kJ; Protein 7.1g; Carbohydrate 66.4g, of which sugars 23.6g; Fat 23.8g, of which saturates 11.7g; Cholesterol 38mg; Calcium 162mg; Fibre 8.6g; Sodium 84mg.

Bread & Butter Pudding

Fresh mixed currants bring a wide-awake character to this scrumptious hot pudding.

ingredients

SERVES SIX

- 8 medium-thick slices day-old bread, crusts removed
- 50g/2oz/¼ cup butter, softened
- 115g/4oz/1 cup redcurrants
- 115g/4oz/1 cup blackcurrants
- 4 eggs, beaten
- 75g/3oz/6 tbsp caster (superfine) sugar
- 475ml/16fl oz/2 cups milk
- 5ml/1 tsp pure vanilla extract
- freshly grated nutmeg
- 30ml/2 tbsp demerara sugar
- single (light) cream, to serve

1 Generously butter a 1.2 litre/2 pint/5 cup baking dish.

2 Butter the slices of bread generously, then cut in half diagonally. Layer the slices in the dish, buttered side up, scattering the currants between the layers.

3 Preheat the oven to 160°C/325°F/Gas 3. Beat the eggs and caster sugar lightly together in a large mixing bowl, then gradually whisk in the milk, vanilla extract and a large pinch of freshly grated nutmeg.

variations

- *To make chocolate bread and butter pudding you can omit the dried fruit and add 150g/5oz chocolate to the milk mixture.*

- *You could replace the dried fruit in either version of the pudding with slices of fresh banana.*

4 Pour the milk mixture over the bread, pushing the slices down. Scatter the demerara sugar and a little nutmeg over the top. Place the dish in a baking tin and fill with hot water to come halfway up the sides of the dish.

5 Bake for 40 minutes, then increase the oven temperature to 180°C/350°F/Gas 4 and bake for approximately 20–25 minutes more or until the top is golden. Allow to cool for a few minutes, then serve with single cream.

NUTRITIONAL INFORMATION: Energy 335kcal/1406kJ; Protein 11.2g; Carbohydrate 41.3g, of which sugars 24.5g; Fat 15.1g, of which saturates 7.6g; Cholesterol 181mg; Calcium 180mg; Fibre 1.3g; Sodium 330mg.

Pecan Pie

This fabulous dessert started life in the United States but has become an international favourite.

ingredients

SERVES FOUR TO SIX

- 115g/4oz/1 cup plain (all-purpose) flour
- 50g/2oz/¼ cup butter, diced
- 25g/1oz/2 tbsp caster (superfine) sugar
- 1 egg yolk

For the filling

- 175g/6oz/5 tbsp golden (light corn) syrup
- 50g/2oz/¼ cup dark muscovado (molasses) sugar
- 50g/2oz/¼ cup butter
- 3 eggs, lightly beaten
- 2.5ml/½ tsp vanilla extract
- 150g/5oz/1¼ cups pecan nuts

1 Place the flour in a bowl and rub the butter into the flour with your fingertips until the mixture resembles breadcrumbs (or use a food processor). Stir in the sugar, egg yolk and about 30ml/2 tbsp cold water. Mix to a dough and knead on a lightly floured surface until smooth.

2 Roll out the pastry and use to line a 20cm/8in fluted loose-based flan tin (pan). Prick the base, then line with baking parchment and fill with baking beans. Chill for 30 minutes. Meanwhile, preheat the oven to 200°C/400°F/Gas 6.

3 Bake the pastry case blind for 10 minutes. Remove the paper and beans and continue to bake for 5 more minutes. Reduce the oven temperature to 180°C/350°F/Gas 4.

4 To make the filling, heat the syrup, sugar and butter in a pan until the sugar dissolves. Remove from the heat and leave to cool slightly. Whisk in the eggs and vanilla extract and stir in the nuts. Pour into the pastry case (pie shell), decorate the top with pecan nuts and bake for 35–40 minutes.

cook's tips

- *Use maple syrup instead of golden syrup to give the filling a more distinctive flavour.*

- *Serve the pie warm with cream or vanilla ice cream.*

NUTRITIONAL INFORMATION: Energy 373kcal/1563kJ; Protein 5.7g; Carbohydrate 51.1g, of which sugars 36.5g; Fat 17.6g, of which saturates 9.8g; Cholesterol 164mg; Calcium 59mg; Fibre 0.6g; Sodium 218mg.

Sherry Trifle

This old-fashioned dessert never fails to please. Make it in a pretty glass dish to show the layers.

ingredients

SERVES SIX

- 75g/3oz day-old sponge (pound) cake, broken into bitesize pieces
- 8 ratafia biscuits (almond macaroons), broken into halves
- 100ml/3½fl oz/⅓ cup medium sherry
- 30ml/2 tbsp brandy
- 350g/12oz/3 cups prepared fruit such as raspberries, peaches or strawberries
- 300ml/½ pint/1¼ cups double (heavy) cream
- 40g/1½oz/scant ½ cup toasted flaked (sliced) almonds, to decorate
- strawberries, to decorate

For the custard

- 4 egg yolks
- 25g/1oz/2 tbsp caster (superfine) sugar
- 450ml/¾ pint/scant 2 cups whipping cream
- a few drops of vanilla extract

1 Put the sponge cake and ratafias in a glass serving dish, then sprinkle over the sherry and brandy and set aside.

2 To make the custard, whisk the egg yolks and caster sugar together. Bring the cream to the boil in a heavy pan, then pour on to the egg yolk mixture, stirring constantly.

3 Return the mixture to the pan and heat very gently, stirring all the time all round the base of the pan with a wooden spoon, until the mixture thickens enough to coat the back of the spoon; do not allow to boil or the custard will curdle. Stir in the vanilla extract and leave to cool, stirring occasionally.

4 Put the fruit in an even layer over the sponge cake and ratafias in the serving dish, then strain the custard over the fruit and leave to set.

5 Lightly whip the cream, then spread it evenly over the surface of the custard. Cover the bowl with clear film (plastic wrap) and chill the trifle well. Decorate the top with a sprinkling of flaked almonds just before serving.

cook's tip

If children will be eating the trifle, you can replace the sherry and brandy with orange juice.

NUTRITIONAL INFORMATION: Energy 764kcal/3160kJ; Protein 7.7g; Carbohydrate 23.2g, of which sugars 17.4g; Fat 68.9g, of which saturates 38.1g; Cholesterol 296mg; Calcium 135mg; Fibre 2.2g; Sodium 106mg.

Summer Pudding

Unbelievably simple to make and totally delicious, this is a real warm weather classic.

ingredients

SERVES FOUR

- about 8 thin slices white bread, at least one day old
- 800g/1¾lb mixed summer fruits
- about 30ml/2 tbsp sugar

4 Cut the remaining bread to fit entirely over the fruit, overlapping it slightly. Stand the bowl on a plate, in case any of the juice overflows the bowl, and cover the top of the pudding with a saucer or small plate that will just fit inside the top of the bowl. Place a heavy weight on top of the saucer. Chill the pudding and the reserved fruit juice overnight.

1 Remove the crusts from the bread. Cut a round from one slice of bread to fit in the base of a 1.2 litre/2 pint/5 cup round, deep bowl and place in position. Cut strips of bread about 5cm/2in wide and use to line the sides of the bowl, overlapping the strips and fitting trimmings into any gaps.

2 Place the fruit, sugar and 30ml/2 tbsp water in a large heavy pan and heat gently, shaking the pan occasionally, until the juices begin to run from the fruit.

3 Reserve about 45ml/3 tbsp fruit juice, then spoon the softened fruit and the remaining juice into the prepared bowl, taking care not to dislodge the pieces of bread lining the sides.

cook's tips

• *Use a good mix of summer fruits for this pudding – red and blackcurrants, raspberries, strawberries and loganberries.*

• *Summer pudding freezes well so make an extra one to enjoy during the winter.*

5 To serve the pudding, run a knife carefully around the inside of the bowl rim, then invert the pudding on to a cold serving plate. Pour over the reserved juice, making sure that all the bread is completely covered, and serve.

NUTRITIONAL INFORMATION: Energy 206kcal/872kJ; Protein 6.2g; Carbohydrate 45.2g, of which sugars 19.9g; Fat 1.2g, of which saturates 0g; Cholesterol 0mg; Calcium 95mg; Fibre 3g; Sodium 293mg.

Raspberry Meringue

A rich, hazelnut meringue sandwiched with cream and raspberries is the ultimate in elegance.

ingredients

SERVES SIX

- 4 egg whites
- 225g/8oz/1 cup caster (superfine) sugar
- a few drops of vanilla extract
- 5ml/1 tsp distilled malt vinegar
- 115g/4oz/1 cup roasted and chopped hazelnuts, ground
- 300ml/½ pint/1¼ cups double (heavy) cream
- 350g/12oz/2 cups raspberries
- icing (confectioners') sugar, for dusting
- fresh mint sprigs, to decorate

For the sauce

- 225g/8oz/1½ cups raspberries
- 45–60ml/3–4 tbsp icing (confectioners') sugar, sifted
- 15ml/1 tbsp orange liqueur

1 Preheat the oven to 180°C/350°F/Gas 4. Grease two 20cm/8in sandwich tins (layer cake pans) and line the bases with baking parchment.

2 Whisk the egg whites in a large clean bowl until they hold stiff peaks, then gradually whisk in the caster sugar a tablespoon at a time, whisking well after each addition. Continue whisking the meringue mixture for a minute of two until very stiff, then fold in the vanilla extract, vinegar and ground hazelnuts.

3 Divide the meringue mixture between the prepared tins and spread lightly with a spatula or palette knife to level the surface. Bake for 50–60 minutes until crisp and golden. Remove the meringues from the tins and leave them to cool on a wire rack.

4 Meanwhile, make the raspberry sauce. Process the raspberries with the icing sugar and liqueur in a blender or food processor, then press through a sieve (strainer) to remove the seeds. Chill the sauce.

5 Whip the cream until it forms soft peaks, then gently fold in the raspberries. Place one meringue round on a serving plate and spread with the raspberry cream. Arrange the other meringue round on top.

6 Dust the top of the meringue thickly with icing sugar and decorate with mint sprigs. Serve the gâteau with the raspberry sauce.

NUTRITIONAL INFORMATION: Energy 434kcal/1799kJ; Protein 6.8g; Carbohydrate 14.3g, of which sugars 13.9g; Fat 39.3g, of which saturates 17.7g; Cholesterol 69mg; Calcium 81mg; Fibre 3.7g; Sodium 56mg.

Iced Chocolate Gâteau

Autumn hazelnuts add crunchiness to this popular iced dinner-party dessert.

ingredients

SERVES SIX TO EIGHT

- 75g/3oz/¾ cup shelled hazelnuts
- about 32 sponge fingers (lady fingers)
- 150ml/¼ pint/⅔ cup cold strong black coffee
- 30ml/2 tbsp Cognac or other brandy
- 450ml/¾ pint/scant 2 cups double (heavy) cream
- 75g/3oz/⅔ cup icing (confectioners') sugar, sifted
- 150g/5oz plain (semisweet) chocolate
- icing (confectioners') sugar and unsweetened cocoa powder, for dusting

1 Preheat the oven to 200°C/400°F/Gas 6. Spread out the hazelnuts on a baking sheet and toast them in the oven for 5 minutes until golden. Transfer the nuts to a clean dish towel and rub off the skins. Cool, then chop finely.

2 Line a 1.2 litre/2 pint/5 cup loaf tin (pan) with clear film (plastic wrap) and cut the sponge fingers to even lengths to fit the base and sides of the loaf tin. (Reserve the remaining fingers to make the top of the gâteau.)

3 Mix the coffee with the brandy in a shallow dish. Dip the sponge fingers into the coffee mixture and arrange in the tin, sugared side down.

4 Whip the cream with the icing sugar until it holds soft peaks. Roughly chop 75g/3oz of the chocolate, and fold into the cream with the hazelnuts.

cook's tip

Take care not to get any water in the chocolate when melting it, as it will become hard and granular.

5 Melt the remaining chocolate in a heatproof bowl set over a pan of barely simmering water. Cool, then fold into the cream mixture. Spoon into the tin.

6 Moisten the remaining sponge fingers in the coffee mixture and lay over the filling. Wrap and freeze until firm.

7 Remove the gâteau from the freezer 30 minutes before serving to soften slightly. Turn out and dust with icing sugar and cocoa powder.

NUTRITIONAL INFORMATION: Energy 631kcal/2628kJ; Protein 8.2g; Carbohydrate 49.7g, of which sugars 38.3g; Fat 44.9g, of which saturates 23.3g; Cholesterol 192mg; Calcium 90mg; Fibre 1.5g; Sodium 57mg.

Chocolate Date Torte

A stunning cake that tastes wonderful. Rich and gooey, it's a chocoholic's delight.

ingredients

SERVES EIGHT

- 4 egg whites
- 115g/4oz/generous ⅔ cup caster (superfine) sugar
- 200g/7oz plain (semisweet) chocolate
- 175g/6oz Medjool dates, stoned (pitted) and chopped
- 175g/6oz/1½ cups walnuts or pecan nuts, chopped
- 5ml/1 tsp vanilla extract

For the frosting

- 200g/7oz/scant 1 cup fromage frais
- 200g/7oz/scant 1 cup mascarpone
- icing (confectioners') sugar, and vanilla extract to taste

1 Preheat the oven to 180°C/350°F/Gas 4. Lightly grease and base-line a 20cm/8in springform cake tin (pan).

2 To make the frosting, mix together the fromage frais and mascarpone, and a few drops of vanilla extract and icing sugar to taste, then set aside.

cook's tip

Medjool dates are succulent with a caramel flavour, perfect for rich, moist cake mixes.

3 Whisk the egg whites in a clean, grease-free bowl until stiff peaks form. Whisk in 30ml/2 tbsp of the caster sugar until the meringue is thick and glossy, then fold in the remaining sugar.

4 Chop 175g/6oz of the chocolate. Carefully fold into the meringue with the dates, nuts and 5ml/1 tsp vanilla extract. Pour the mixture into the prepared tin, level the surface lightly and bake for about 45 minutes, until risen around the edges.

5 Allow the torte to cool in the tin for about 10 minutes, then turn out on to a wire rack. Peel off the lining paper and leave until completely cold. When cool, swirl the frosting over the top of the torte.

6 To decorate, melt the remaining chocolate in a bowl set over hot water. Spoon into a small paper piping (pastry) bag, snip off the tip and drizzle the chocolate over the frosting. Chill the torte in the refrigerator before serving, cut into wedges.

NUTRITIONAL INFORMATION: Energy 427kcal/1784kJ; Protein 9.2g; Carbohydrate 41.5g, of which sugars 40.9g; Fat 26g, of which saturates 7.8g; Cholesterol 12mg; Calcium 57mg; Fibre 2.1g; Sodium 41mg.

Chocolate Eclairs

These choux pastry éclairs are filled with a luscious vanilla-flavoured cream.

1 Preheat the oven to 200°C/400°F/Gas 6. Grease a large baking sheet and line with a sheet of baking parchment.

2 To make the choux pastry, sift the flour with the salt on to a small sheet of baking parchment. Very gently heat the butter and 150ml/¼ pint/²/₃ cup water in a pan until the butter has melted. Bring to a rolling boil, then remove from the heat and immediately add all the flour. Beat vigorously with a wooden spoon to mix well.

3 Return the pan to a low heat. Beat the mixture until it leaves the sides of the pan and forms a ball. Set aside and allow to cool for 2–3 minutes.

4 Beat in the eggs, a little at a time, to form a smooth, shiny paste. Spoon into a piping (pastry) bag fitted with a 2.5cm/1in plain nozzle.

5 Pipe 10cm/4in lengths on to the baking sheet. Bake for 25–30 minutes, or until the pastries are well risen and golden brown.

6 Make a neat slit along the side of each éclair to release the steam. Lower the temperature to 180°C/350°F/Gas 4 and bake for a further 5 minutes. Cool on a wire rack.

7 To make the filling, whip the cream with the icing sugar and vanilla until it just holds its shape. Pipe into the éclairs.

8 Place the chocolate and 30ml/2 tbsp water in a small bowl over a pan of hot water. Melt, stirring, then remove from the heat and gradually stir in the butter. Coat the éclairs with the chocolate mixture. Leave on a rack to set.

NUTRITIONAL INFORMATION: Energy 253kcal/1046kJ; Protein 2.7g; Carbohydrate 10.8g, of which sugars 6.5g; Fat 22.4g, of which saturates 13.5g; Cholesterol 86mg; Calcium 30mg; Fibre 0.4g; Sodium 58mg.

Crème Brûlée

This classic brûlée dish can be made in advance and tastes delicious.

ingredients

SERVES SIX

- 1 vanilla pod (bean)
- 1 litre/1¾ pints/4 cups double (heavy) cream
- 6 egg yolks
- 90g/3½oz/½ cup caster (superfine) sugar
- 30ml/2 tbsp almond or orange liqueur (optional)
- 75g/3oz/6 tbsp sugar

variation

For a lighter version of the same dish, replace the double cream with a 300g/11oz packet of silken tofu and add some soft berry fruits to the bottom of each ramekin.

1 Preheat the oven to 150°C/300°F/Gas 2. Place six 120ml/4fl oz/½ cup ramekins, in a roasting pan and set aside.

2 Split the vanilla pod (bean) lengthways and scrape the black seeds into a pan. Add the cream and bring to the boil, stirring. Take from the heat and cover. Set aside for 15–20 minutes.

cook's tip

If you do not have a vanilla pod (bean), you can use 1 teaspoon of vanilla extract instead.

3 In a bowl, whisk the egg yolks, caster sugar and liqueur, if using. Whisk in the hot cream and strain into a jug (pitcher). Divide the custard among the ramekins. Pour enough boiling water into the roasting pan to come halfway up the sides of the ramekins.

4 Cover the pan with foil and bake for about 30 minutes until the custards are just set. Remove from the pan and leave to cool. Return to the dry roasting pan and chill the custards until ready to serve.

5 Preheat the grill (boiler). Sprinkle the sugar evenly over the surface of each custard and grill (broil) for 30–60 seconds until the sugar melts and caramelizes. Place in the refrigerator to set the crust and chill before serving.

NUTRITIONAL INFORMATION: Energy 996cal/4116kJ; Protein 5.7g; Carbohydrate 31.6g, of which sugars 95g; Fat 3.2g, of which saturates 57.2g; Cholesterol 430mg; Calcium 120mg; Fibre 0g; Sodium 47mg.

Cookies & Cream

Rich, smooth and packed with cookies, this heavenly ice cream is a real treat.

ingredients

SERVES FOUR TO SIX

- 4 egg yolks
- 90ml/6 tbsp sugar
- 5ml/1 tsp cornstarch
- 300ml/½ pint/1¼ cups skimmed (low-fat) milk
- 5ml/1 tsp vanilla extract
- 300ml/½ pint/1¼ cups whipping cream
- 150g/5oz/1¼ cups chunky chocolate and hazelnut cookies, crumbled into medium-sized pieces

1 Whisk the egg yolks, sugar and cornstarch in a bowl until the mixture is thick and foamy. Pour the milk into a heavy pan, bring it just to a boil, then pour it onto the yolk mixture, whisking constantly.

2 Return to the pan and cook over a low heat, stirring continuously until the custard thickens and it is smooth. Pour the custard back into the bowl and cover closely. Allow the mixture to cool and then place in the refrigerator to chill for about 30 minutes.

3 Stir the vanilla into the custard. Whip the cream until it is thickened but still soft.

cook's tip

Experiment with different cookies to achieve the best results.

4 Carefully fold the cream into the chilled custard, then pour into a plastic or other freezerproof container. Freeze for 4 hours, beating once with a fork, electric beater or in a food processor to break up the ice crystals. Beat one more time, then fold in the crumbled-up cookie chunks. Cover tightly and return to the freezer until firm.

NUTRITIONAL INFORMATION: Energy 428kcal/1782kJ; Protein 6.2g; Carbohydrate 36.3g, of which sugars 27.1g; Fat 29.7g, of which saturates 16.4g; Cholesterol 189mg; Calcium 135mg; Fibre 0.5g; Sodium 129mg.

Lemon Sorbet

Refreshingly tangy and yet deliciously smooth, this has to be the classic sorbet.

ingredients

SERVES SIX

- 200g/7oz/1 cup caster (superfine) sugar
- 300ml/1/2 pint/1¼ cups water
- 4 lemons, well scrubbed
- 1 egg white
- sugared lemon rind, to decorate (see cook's tip)

cook's tip

To make sugared lemon rind, thinly pare the rind with a zester. Dust with a little caster (superfine) sugar.

1 Put the sugar and water into a pan and bring to the boil over a low heat, stirring until the sugar has just dissolved.

2 Using a vegetable peeler pare the rind thinly from two of the lemons so that it falls straight into the pan.

3 Simmer for about 2 minutes, without stirring, then take the pan off the heat. Leave to cool, then chill.

4 Squeeze the juice from the lemons and add to the syrup. Strain the syrup into a shallow freezerproof container.

5 Reserve the rind. Freeze the mixture for 4 hours, until it is mushy. If you are using an ice cream maker, strain the syrup and lemon juice and then churn the mixture until thick.

6 Scoop the sorbet into a food processor and beat it until smooth. Lightly whisk the egg white with a fork until it is just frothy. Spoon the sorbet back into the container, beat in the egg white to the mixture and continue to churn for 10–15 minutes, or until the sorbet is firm enough to scoop.

7 Scoop the sorbet into bowls, decorate with sugared lemon rind and serve.

NUTRITIONAL INFORMATION: Energy 135kcal/574kJ; Protein 0.7g; Carbohydrate 35.1g, of which sugars 33.8g; Fat 0g, of which saturates 0g; Cholesterol 0mg; Calcium 19mg; Fibre 0g; Sodium 12mg.

COOK'S NOTES

Bracketed terms are intended for American readers.

For all recipes, quantities are given in both metric and imperial measures and, where appropriate, in standard cups and spoons. Follow one set of measures, but not a mixture, because they are not interchangeable.

Standard spoon and cup measures are level. 1 tsp = 5ml, 1 tbsp = 15ml, 1 cup = 250ml/8fl oz.

Australian standard tablespoons are 20ml. Australian readers should use 3 tsp in place of 1 tbsp for measuring small quantities.

American pints are 16fl oz/2 cups. American readers should use 20fl oz/2.5 cups in place of 1 pint when measuring liquids.

Electric oven temperatures in this book are for conventional ovens. When using a fan oven, the temperature will probably need to be reduced by about 10–20°C/20–40°F. Since ovens vary, you should check with your manufacturer's instruction book for guidance.

The nutritional analysis given for each recipe is calculated per portion (i.e. serving or item), unless otherwise stated. If the recipe gives a range, such as Serves 4–6, then the nutritional analysis will be for the smaller portion size, i.e. 6 servings. Measurements for sodium do not include salt added to taste.

Medium (US large) eggs are used unless otherwise stated.

This edition is published by Lorenz Books,
an imprint of Anness Publishing Ltd, Blaby Road,
Wigston, Leicestershire, LE18 4SE
www.annesspublishing.com

If you like the images in this book and would like to investigate using them for publishing, promotions or advertising, please visit our website www.practicalpictures.com
for more information.